SIGMUND
FREUD

THE MAN, THE SCIENTIST, AND THE BIRTH OF PSYCHOANALYSIS

RUTH SHEPPARD

ROSEN
PUBLISHING

New York

Published in 2022 by The Rosen Publishing Group, Inc.
29 East 21st Street, New York, NY 10010

Published in 2019 by Andre Deutsch, a division of the Carlton Publishing Group.
Design copyright © Carlton Books 2019. Text copyright © Ruth Sheppard 2019.

Cataloging-in-Publication Data

Names: Sheppard, Ruth.
Title: Sigmund Freud / Ruth Sheppard.
Description: New York : Rosen YA, 2022. | Series: Pioneers of science
Identifiers: ISBN 9781499471182 (pbk.) | ISBN 9781499471199 (library bound) |
ISBN 9781499471205 (ebook)
Subjects: LCSH: Freud, Sigmund, 1856-1939--Juvenile literature. |
Psychoanalysts--Austria--Biography--Juvenile literature.
Classification: LCC BF173.F85 S48 2022 | DDC 150.19'52092 B--dc23

Manufactured in the United States of America

CPSIA Compliance Information: Batch #CSRYA22.
For Further Information contact Rosen Publishing, New York, New York at 1-800-237-9932.

Find us on

Contents

Foreword

This unique book is written as if one were standing in Freud's study and consulting room as he left it in 1939. On the shelves are the books he read in science, art, literature, history, archaeology, and psychology. The antiquities he loved are displayed on every surface and in glass cabinets, testifying not only to the importance of "the past" in his work, but to the breadth of his cultural interests. Portraits of the people he admired are hung on the walls and shelves – his former teachers and colleagues, and the women who shared his life. Lined against the wall is the iconic couch on which hundreds of patients recounted thousands of dreams and memories, following the rule of free association. *Freud* recreates this setting in its illustrated presentation and by doing so poses the question that gets to the heart of the Freud biographer's quest: "Where did Freud's ideas come from?"

To explore further we are given privileged access into the archive of letters, photographs and documents held at the Freud Museum. The documents and photographs add color to the book, creating a truly "graphic" biography which succeeds in making Freud come alive in the text. It is perhaps not surprising that the author herself has written exhibition material for national museums. Framed within the context of political developments in Europe, the impact of anti-Semitism, industrialization, and developments in biology, medicine, and psychiatry, we see Freud as a researcher worried about his career, who falls in love, makes mistakes (and writes about them), worries about his health and money and friendships, whose adult life was gripped by a passionate desire to discover the "secrets of the soul" and who left a legacy that continues to this day. The structure of the book facilitates this multidimensional and multilayered approach. A main text is complemented by images and captions that provide a different level of information; short biographies of other "key players" (psychologists, colleagues, patients, friends) are distributed in separate "windows"; facsimiles of key archive documents are provided in special pockets to remove and examine. One of the most compelling of these is the handwritten text of Freud's broadcast for the BBC in 1938 in which he summarizes his professional life in less than 120 words. As a piece of writing it is succinct enough for any modern tweeter to be proud.

Freud has been much criticized in recent years and critics have often used the ambiguous term "Freud" to elide the difference between the "man" and his "work." *Ad hominem* arguments are standard fare for the average Freud critic, presenting his ideas as nothing more than the product of a "neurotic personality." As a popular and accessible account, this book will open up a new picture of Freud for many people, showing "the man Freud" in the context of his times, his work, his friends, his colleagues, and his family. There is much to discover here and much to admire as an illustrated account of the life of Freud.

Ivan Ward, Director of Education, and Carol Seigel, Director at the Freud Museum, London

Introduction

The ideas of the Austrian psychoanalyst Sigmund Freud pepper our everyday conversation, used correctly or otherwise: "Was that a Freudian slip?" "You're repressing your emotions." "He has such a big ego." His influence has undeniably pervaded Western culture and thought, yet the man himself is – as he always has been – often misunderstood and ridiculed, crudely caricatured as a pervert obsessed with sex, cigar in hand, perched on a chair next to a gullible or vulnerable patient on a couch.

Over the seven decades since his death, not all of his theories have stood the test of time, many of them undergoing revision, or rejection, and today only very few comprehend the astonishing achievement he made. Alone, and against strong criticism, the young doctor forged an entirely new discipline, born out of a desire to create a better way of treating his patients. While those who have heard of Freud may know something of the Oedipus complex or his other sexual theories – most of which are still controversial – very few are aware of the sheer volume and breadth of work that this great mind produced over six decades. Even as early as the 1890s, Freud's ambition was nothing less than to create a new psychology, to try and map the minds of not only those suffering neurotic illnesses, but of everyone. He became one of the greatest intellectuals of the nineteenth and twentieth centuries, and his work ranged from the scientific and neurological texts of his youth, through his major psychoanalytic books, to writings on religion, society, art, and culture.

Freud introduces Sigmund Freud the man and the scientist, the husband and father, the pioneering psychoanalyst and creator and leader of an international community of analysts. Tracing his life from childhood in a complex family, through his

medical training to the independent path he then trod toward the creation of psychoanalysis, we then examine his major theories and concepts, which he continued to develop until old age, even as he was dying of cancer. The selection of Freud's case notes and theories, letters and diary entries, some of them in his own handwriting, allow us to get even closer to the man himself, as do the lavish selection of illustrations, showing Freud, his family, colleagues, and followers. Together, these elements offer an insight into the life and works of the greatest "explorer of the mind."

PAGE 4 *Freud at his desk in his temporary accommodation in Elsworth Road.*

ABOVE *Freud tended to write late every evening and into the small hours, only working on his new theories and books after a full day of analysis, writing up notes for each patient and replying to correspondence.*

The World Before Freud

Sigmund Freud was born in Moravia on May 6, 1856, then under the rule of the Empire of Austria, into a rapidly changing world. The Holy Roman Empire had been dissolved under Napoleon Bonaparte (1769–1821) in 1806, but in anticipation of losing his powers, Emperor Francis II (1768–1835) had declared himself Emperor of Austria. The empire emerged from the Napoleonic Wars as one of the dominant powers of Europe. Austria and Prussia were the main powers in the

German confederation formed after the Congress of Vienna in 1815. Despite the efforts of the major players to restore the balance of power in Europe, the years after the Napoleonic Wars saw the spread of revolutionary movements.

In 1848, revolutions within the German confederation sought to create a unified German state. The confederation was briefly dissolved, then re-established in 1850. Then, while Freud was still a young boy, Austria and Prussia would come to blows

ABOVE *The united Prussian armies defeated the main Austrian army at the Battle of Sadowa (also known as Königgrätz) in July 1866,* *and decided the outcome of the Austro-Prussian War, with an armistice signed three weeks later.*

socio-economic and cultural consequences. Huge advances in technology, such as steam power, powered machinery, and improvements in road, rail, and water transport revolutionized all aspects of life. Not everyone would benefit from this process; in their small country town in Moravia, Freud's family would suffer financially from the fallout of these advances, and as part of the town's Jewish community they would also be made scapegoats for others' misfortune. Thus, anti-Semitism affected Freud's life from the very beginning, and would haunt him his entire life until he was forced to leave his home and flee from the Nazis as a sick, elderly man.

Medicine was one of the disciplines that changed beyond recognition during the nineteenth century, including the categorization and treatment of

ABOVE *Street fighting over the National Government in Frankfurt in 1848. The March Revolution in Vienna caused uprising throughout all of Germany. In May 1848, the Frankfurt Assembly was convened, the first freely elected parliament for all Germany.*

RIGHT *Franz Joseph I (1830–1916) was Emperor of Austria, King of Bohemia, King of Croatia, and Apostolic King of Hungary for 68 years, ascending the throne after the abdication of his uncle and renunciation of his father.*

over the right to rule German lands. The outcome of the Austro-Prussian War of 1866 was a Prussian victory. The confederation collapsed and the North German Confederation was created, with a number of southern German states later becoming the nation of Germany. The following year the Austro-Hungarian Compromise led to a dual sovereignty, with the Austrian Empire and Kingdom of Hungary ruled by Franz Joseph I (1830–1916).

As well as political change, a wave of industrialization emanating from the Industrial Revolution in Great Britain spread throughout Europe during the nineteenth century and had far-reaching

mental illness. Interest in the mind and behavior dates back to ancient times, and there is evidence of psychiatric treatment for those with mental illnesses in eighth-century Islamic asylums. While asylums had existed for centuries, the institutionalization of those with mental illnesses was very much an eighteenth- and nineteenth-century phenomenon. There was an increase in the number of people diagnosed with mental illness during this period, which can be attributed to a number of factors, including the strain put on families by industrialization, and also a lower tolerance for unusual behavior by society because there was now a valid option of sending people who didn't conform away to an asylum.

Many asylums became large, impersonal institutions teeming with people afflicted by mental and socio-economic problems. Though there were exceptions, many asylums were dirty, disgusting, and depressing places, where "patients" were restrained, or paraded in front of the public. Around the turn of the nineteenth century, treatment of those

in asylums began to improve. In Paris, Philippe Pinel (1745–1826) instituted huge changes at the Bicêtre asylum for men in the 1790s, unchaining the patients, giving them decent accommodation, and occupying them with simple work tasks. Pinel called this moral therapy. He spent hours with the patients, and through talking to them created detailed case histories for them all. He refused to allow bleeding, purging, and blistering in his hospital. Until the mid-nineteenth century, many mentally ill patients would receive similar "moral treatment," but many in the medical profession began to argue that the mentally ill also had physical problems, and medical treatment was therefore also necessary.

The term "psychiatry" was coined in 1808, replacing the older term "alienism." The discipline developed as the asylums proliferated, leading to significant improvements in the treatment of the mentally ill. Germany became known as the world leader in psychiatry during the nineteenth century. Its universities produced psychiatrists competing

" *...deep within me... there continues to live the happy child from Freiberg.* **"**

– SIGMUND FREUD

OPPOSITE *Depiction of an asylum in Spain (c. 1812–1819) by Francisco de Goya. Psychiatric institutions were much discussed in Spain at this time, and this painting could be intended as a denunciation of contemporary practices.*

ABOVE *Mesmer developed a collective treatment where iron rods protruding from a "baquet" touched his patients' afflicted parts while he "conveyed the fluid" with hand and eye motions.*

to advance treatments and understanding of illnesses of the mind.

Many different theories and treatments were developed to help the mentally ill, such as Mesmerism, the precursor to hypnosis. Franz Anton Mesmer (1734–1815) was an Austrian physician who asserted that a magnetic fluid resided in animate beings. It flowed through the body, and was affected by the currents in other bodies. He called this "animal magnetism." A deficiency of animal magnetism, or obstructions to the flow of the mysterious fluids in the body, caused illness. Contact with a conductor of "animal magnetism" would effect a cure. It became a popular theory, widely practiced, with the techniques becoming secret. Many were sceptical, calling animal magnetism quackery. A French royal commission into his treatments, ordered by Louis XVI (1754–1793) in 1784, found there to be no evidence of the existence of Mesmer's magnetic fluid, and that the effects he achieved had been derived from the imagination or trickery. One of his disciples, Abbé Faria (1746–1819), continued with Mesmer's work, conducting experiments to show that the trances and other phenomena caused through mesmeric techniques were created by the power of suggestion.

Scottish surgeon James Braid (1795–1860) observed demonstrations of mesmerism in 1841, examining the mesmerized subjects, and concluding that they were in a different physical state. Braid began to experiment with his own method, a "rational mesmerism," which resulted in the development of neurohypnotism (nervous sleep), which was based upon physiological and psychological principles. A hypnotic state could be induced through staring at an object with fixed attention for a prolonged time. Braid rejected any suggestion that it was the power of the practitioner, or the imagination of the subject, that caused the hypnotic state. His work influenced several French medical figures, including the neurologist Jean-Martin Charcot (1825–1893).

Vienna, the city where Freud would live most of his life and make many of his important discoveries into the mind, already had a reputation for developments in medicine, particularly psychiatry. The Narrenturm in Vienna is Europe's oldest building for the accommodation of mental patients. Its construction in 1784 was prompted by the discovery of mentally ill Capuchin brethren being kept in underground dungeons. Adjacent to the old Vienna General Hospital, the Narrenturm housed 200 to 250 mental patients. Each cell had rings for restraining patients. Within a decade, it was outdated owing to developments in treatment for patients with mental illnesses. Many specialist clinics were established in Vienna from the late eighteenth century, and the first psychiatric

William James (1842–1910)

James studied medicine at Harvard, but never practiced. As a young man he was diagnosed as a neurasthenic and travelled to Germany, where his search for a cure led him to focus on psychology and philosophy. He spent almost his entire academic career at Harvard, teaching physiology, anatomy, psychology, and philosophy. He was endowed with the chair in psychology in 1889. His connections with men like Hermann Helmholtz and Pierre Janet led to his introducing courses in scientific psychology at Harvard, and he started teaching experimental psychology there in 1875. His students included Granville Stanley Hall and Theodore Roosevelt. He was a strong proponent of the school of functionalism in psychology, and wrote influential books on psychology, educational psychology, and philosophy.

clinic in Austria was founded at the Vienna asylum in 1870. Vienna had an array of asylums and therapies for all mental illnesses. The Viennese psychiatric approach was mainly concerned with physical symptoms, and family pathology. There was not much interest in the underlying causes of mental illnesses.

The word "psychology" came into usage in the mid-nineteenth century. Previously known as "mind philosophy," the term evolved as it transformed from a study of the soul to a medical discipline. Psychology as a field of experimental study developed in 1879, when Wilhelm Wundt (1832–1920) founded the first laboratory dedicated to psychological research in Leipzig. In his lab he identified mental disorders and abnormal behavior, mapping damaged areas of the brain.

Freud would come into this fast-paced and exciting world of discoveries as a meticulous scientist, and trained physician. He would create a new branch of science, a new psychology that not only tried to explain and alleviate mental illnesses, but in his own words, to form "a new and deeper science of the mind which would be … indispensable for the understanding of the normal."

Wilhelm Wundt (1832–1920)

Wilhelm Wundt, German doctor, physiologist, psychologist, and philosopher, is widely regarded as the father of experimental psychology. Wundt was an assistant to Hermann von Helmholtz, whose sensory physiology was the basis of Wundt's work. He was also influenced by Gustav Theodor Fechner, an early pioneer in experimental psychology. In 1874 he published *Principles of Physiological Psychology*, which came to be one of the most important works in the history of psychology. He founded the first laboratory for psychological research at the Universität of Leipzig in 1879. Through his work there, he was able to establish psychology as a separate science.

Freud's Childhood

Sigmund Freud knew from a young age that he was destined for greatness. Born the eldest child of Jakob (1815–1896) and Amalia (1835–1930) Freud, much was expected of him by his family, and on many occasions the needs and wishes of the eldest son would be openly preferred over those of their other children. Moreover, in the exciting years of the mid-nineteenth century there seemed to be a lot of possibilities for a bright young man to succeed in science or art, and Freud happily shared his family's expectations. He was born with a caul, which was thought to ensure his future happiness and fame. His mother's hopes for his bright future were further strengthened when an old lady she met in a pastry shop informed her that she had brought a great man into the world. When Freud was 11 or 12, a poet in a restaurant improvized a verse about him, declaring he would probably grow up to be a cabinet minister, which Sigmund thought quite possible at the time, even if he would later realize that anti-Semitism would complicate the future of any Jew in a prominent position in Austrian public life.

Sigismund Schlomo Freud was born in Freiberg, Moravia (then under Habsburg rule, now Příbor, Czech Republic) on May 6, 1856. Schlomo was the name of his paternal grandfather, who died a few months before his birth. Freud was known to his family as "Sigi," and chose to abbreviate his given name to Sigmund in 1877.

Jakob's family, who were Orthodox Jews, had fled east centuries before to escape a persecution of the Jews, and had migrated back from Lithuania through Galicia into German Austria during the nineteenth century. Freud's father was a merchant, mainly trading in wool. By the late 1850s, Freiberg was a town in steep decline, with huge unemployment. Not only was Jakob's business affected, but the Czech nationalism established

LEFT *Freud's hometown of Příbor-Freiberg. A memorial plaque was placed on the house where he was born in 1931, and Freud wrote a letter to thank those organizing the honor.*

following the 1848–1849 revolution led to an inclination to blame the town's community of Jews, who were mainly German in language and education, for the economic mess the small town found itself in. Jakob realized there was no future for his family in Freiberg, and the family moved to Leipzig, staying there a year before settling in Vienna.

Freud was not born into a straightforward nuclear family. His father was 20 years older than his mother. He had been married before, and his two grown sons, Emanuel and Philipp, and their families, lived near to the Freud family. Amalia was younger than Emanuel, and still a teenager when she married Jakob. Sigmund was born an uncle, as Emanuel had a son, John, who was a year older than Sigmund. The two boys were

TOP RIGHT *Freud aged seven, sitting at a desk. Even at this age, Freud's studies were given priority by his family, and his siblings knew not to disturb him.*

ABOVE *A bird's-eye view of Vienna in 1860. Freud's family moved to the Jewish quarter of Vienna in 1859. Freud would always have an ambivalent attitude to the city, seeming to love and hate it in equal measure, not least because of the prevalent anti-Semitism.*

constant playmates until Emanuel moved his family to England when Sigmund was three. As with many small children, their relationship alternated between affection and hatred, and though younger, Sigmund gave as good as he got when the two fought. In later life Sigmund would consider that his often turbulent friendships, particularly those with men of a similar age, stemmed from his ambivalent relationship with his nephew. He felt that an intimate friend and hated enemy were always indispensable to his emotional life, and in fact on several occasions this turned out to exist in the same person, though not at the same time. He commented to his friend Wilhelm Fliess (1858–1928, see Chapter 7) that his nephew and younger brother had determined "what [was] neurotic, but also what [was] intense" in all his friendships.

It must have been confusing to the young Freud that John, older and stronger, was his nephew, and that he called Freud's father "grandfather." As Emanuel remarked to Freud when the latter was a teenager, there were really three generations in the family. Freud's self-analysis in his forties (see Chapter 11) led him to realize that perhaps owing to his confusing family dynamics, as a boy he had created a fantasy that his half-brother Philipp had had an affair with his mother, which had resulted

❝ *The act of birth is the first experience of anxiety, and thus the source and prototype of the affect of anxiety.* **❞**

– SIGMUND FREUD

his mother's love and attention had to be shared, and that Julius' death then provoked feelings of self-reproach.

The couple's first daughter, Anna, arrived when Freud was two and a half. Anna was followed by Rosa, Marie (Mitzi), Adolfine (Dolfi), and Paula. The Freuds' youngest child, Alexander, was just 10 years younger than Freud.

At the time his sister Anna was born, Freud's elderly Czech nanny was dismissed for theft. He had been very fond of the old lady, who conversed with him in Czech, and regularly took him to Roman Catholic church services, introducing him to the ideas of heaven and hell. After returning from church he would preach a sermon at home. The nanny had, like his parents, given Freud reason to think very highly of his own abilities. The distressing memory of the dismissal was recalled during self-analysis of his dreams many years later, and verified by his mother.

Freud was just three years old when the family left Freiburg. The journey away from his home prompted the beginnings of a travel anxiety. He also indicated in later life that the anxiety may

in his sister Anna. Given that Amalia and Philipp were almost the same age, this must have seemed quite plausible to the young boy, and perhaps shows that the family composition was quite puzzling to a small child, though there is no indication that his fantasy was in any way based on truth.

Amalia was 21 when she gave birth to Sigmund. She was born Amalia Nathansohn, in north-east Galicia, in 1835. She spent some of her childhood in Odessa and in Vienna, where she was an eyewitness to the 1848 revolution. After Sigmund, Amalia and Jakob went on to have seven more children in swift succession. Her next child, Julius, died at the age of eight months, when Sigmund was only 19 months old. He later admitted he felt jealousy toward his younger brother because

ABOVE *A Vienna synagogue in the 1860s. Despite his "unbelief," Freud felt himself to be thoroughly Jewish, and was sensitive to any anti-Semitism, which was in fact rife in nineteenth-century Vienna.*

have been related to seeing his mother naked on an overnight train journey from Leipzig to Vienna while he was still a small boy. Even after he had overcome the phobia, he retained an anxiety about catching trains, often arriving at the station as much as an hour early. Leaving the childhood home where he had been happy must have been difficult for the young boy, and he seems to have remembered the small town and the countryside around it with continuing affection. At around the same time as Jakob took his family east, both Freud's half-brothers

ABOVE *The Rotunda in the Prater (park) for the Vienna World Fair in 1873. Its motto was Kultur und Erziehung (Culture and Education).*

emigrated to Manchester, England, so Freud also lost his playmate John.

When Freud was 16, he made his only visit to his place of birth. He stayed with family friends, the Fluss family, and promptly fell in love with the daughter, Gisela, who was slightly younger than him. Too shy to speak to her, he wandered in the woods, wondering how much more enjoyable his life would have been had his parents stayed in Freiberg, where he would have grown up a country lad and married Gisela.

The first few years in Vienna were tough ones for Jakob and his young family, and they lived for a time in a small apartment on the Pfeffergasse, a street in the quarter of Leopoldstädt, where many of Vienna's Jews lived in overcrowded dwellings. It is unlikely the family kept up their Orthodox customs after they moved to Vienna perhaps partly because their cramped accommodation did not allow proper observance of certain customs, such as the keeping of a kosher kitchen. The growing family soon needed more room, and moved to a flat on the Kaiser Josefstrasse. It had a living room, dining room, kitchen, three bedrooms, and a "cabinet," a long narrow room separate from the rest of the flat. There was no bathroom, and baths would be taken once a fortnight in a large wooden tub in the kitchen. The cabinet was given to the young Freud, who lived there until he was working and studying at the Vienna General Hospital. Unlike the other bedrooms, which were lit by candles, Freud had an oil lamp, with which to better illuminate his hours of study. As a teenager he ate his evening meals in his room, so as not to waste time away from his books. His parents' dedication to supporting the

answer questions in class. He was dedicated to his education, with reading and studying taking up the majority of his time.

He was gifted at languages, mastering Latin, Greek, French, English, Italian, and Spanish, as well as Hebrew. He was especially fond of English, and admired the works of Shakespeare, which he had begun reading at the age of eight. In turn, he helped his sisters with their studies. He seems to have been quite an authoritative older brother, censoring what was appropriate for his sisters to read, and giving them advice on how they should behave.

At school, Freud made a close friend, Eduard Silberstein (1856–1925), with whom he would maintain an intimate correspondence throughout their teens and twenties. They taught themselves Spanish and formed what Freud described as a "strange scholarly society," the Academia Castallana. They corresponded in Spanish, using secret names and jokes. They drifted apart after Freud met his wife.

In 1873, Freud passed his Matura (school leaving certificate) with distinction at the age of 17. His father promised him a trip to England as a reward for his achievement. He was 19 when he visited his half-brothers in the country for which he had already cultivated a fondness, an affection that would last throughout his life.

Freud's parents had both been raised Orthodox Jews. Freud was circumcised as a baby, and knew all the Jewish customs and festivals. The family observed the Seder on the eve of Passover, along with Christmas and Easter. In his autobiographical essay of 1924, Freud stated that he remained a Jew. Most of his friends were Jews, and he was sensitive to the slightest hint of anti-Semitism, which he would have encountered from childhood in Vienna, but he commented to friend Oskar Pfister

rise of their son was such that when he felt his study was disturbed by his younger sister's piano playing, the piano was removed from the flat at his request, even though his mother was very musical.

Freud was initially taught by his mother, then his education was taken over by his father before he was sent to private school. When he was nine he took an examination, and upon passing was allowed to attend high school a year earlier than his contemporaries. So, in 1865, Freud entered the Leopoldstädter Kommunal-Realgymnasium. After the first two years, he was constantly at the top of his class. He was said to enjoy a privileged position in the school, and was rarely expected to

(1873–1956), a Lutheran pastor, that he was a "godless Jew." However, on his 35th birthday, Freud was given a bible by his father, with an inscription in Hebrew. Freud read the Bible as a child, and later said he was greatly influenced by it, though it is unclear whether this was in a religious sense, or in ethical and historical senses. (See also Chapter 18.)

Even when Freud was a teenager, the family was not well off, yet Jakob insisted that Freud choose his own career path regardless of financial considerations. The career options facing him as a Viennese Jew were industry, business, law, or medicine. Influenced by an older school friend, Freud developed a wish to study the law. However, just before leaving school he changed his mind. Darwin's writings were at the time topical, and Freud was very attracted by them, and the possibilities they seemed to suggest for a greater understanding of the world. He himself said that he didn't particularly want to be a doctor, but he was inspired to consider medicine by a curiosity about human concerns. He finally made up his mind to study medicine after hearing Goethe's essay on nature just before leaving school.

ABOVE *The apartment block in Vienna where Freud lived.*

Maturitäts-Zeugnis.

Freud Sigmund aus Freiberg

in Mähren geboren am 6. Mai 1856

hat die Gymnasialstudien ohne Unterbrechung am Leo-

poldstädter Comm.Real- und Obergymn.

in den Jahren 1865–1873 beendige, und sich der Maturitäts-Prüfung vor der

unterzeichneten Prüfungs-Kommission unterworfen.

Auf Grund derselben wird ihm nachstehendes Zeugnis ausgestellt:

Sittliches Betragen:

Leistungen in den einzelnen Prüfungs-Gegenständen:

Religionslehre: vorzüglich

Lateinische Sprache: vorzüglich

Geriechische Sprache: _vorzüglich_

Deutsche Sprache: _ausgezeichnet_

Geschichte und Geographie: _vorzüglich_

Mathematik: _vorzüglich_

Physik
Naturwissenschaften: _vorzüglich_

philosophische Propädeutik: _vorzüglich_

Allgemeine Naturkunde: _lobenswert_

Da hiernach der Examinand den gesetzlichen Forderungen _mit Auszeichnung_ entsprochen hat, so wird ihm hiedurch das

Zeugnis der Reife zum Besuche einer Universität

ausgestellt.

Wien am 9. Juli 1873.

This is the record of Freud's Matura, or school leaving certificate, which he took in 1873. It shows the subjects he studied, and the high level of attainment he achieved in all of them.

Medical School

Freud entered **Vienna University** as a student of medicine in 1873 aged just 17. The open curriculum at the university allowed him to pursue his wider interests, and he admitted that he preferred this approach over one of covering the areas strictly necessary to complete his medical training, even though it took him three years longer than necessary to qualify.

For the first three semesters he took a broad range of classes, but in the summer of 1875 he began to branch out. Instead of attending "zoology for medical students," he chose the zoology proper lectures. He also took more courses than strictly necessary in physics, philosophy, and physiology. The following year he moved further toward biology,

ABOVE *Vienna University in the nineteenth century.*

spending 10 hours a week in the practical zoology laboratory of Professor Karl Claus (1835–1899), alongside his physiology, anatomy, and philosophy.

In March 1876 he began his first original research. Karl Claus gave him a grant to study at the university's zoology experimental station in Trieste, a decision reflecting well on Freud's work and conduct. The research concerned the gonads of eels. Freud dissected around 400 eels. He found an organ which might have been an immature testicular organ, but no definitive evidence that it was. He was very dissatisfied with his inconclusive results. Between his visits to Trieste that summer, Freud concentrated on biology, taking the majority of his classes in zoology.

In the autumn of 1876, Freud was accepted into the Institute of Physiology as a *famulus*, a research scholar. The Institute was the domain of Ernst Brücke (1819–1892), who would prove to be the most important teacher in Freud's life. Freud had attended physiology lectures given by Brücke since his first semester, but he recalled that, after three years at university, he felt he finally found rest and satisfaction in Brücke's laboratory, and men he could respect in Brücke and his assistants, Sigmund Exner (1846–1926) and Ernst von Fleischl-Marxow (1846–1891).

Brücke was a stern, quiet man. Though rational and austere, he was considerate toward his able pupils, respecting their ideas, encouraging original work, and supporting their talents even if he did not agree with their ideas. In the 1840s, Brücke and Emil du Bois-Reymond (1818–1896), along with Hermann Helmholtz (1821–1894) and Carl Ludwig (1816–1895), began a far-reaching movement,

Joseph Breuer (1842–1925)

Freud first met Breuer while working in Brücke's lab. Breuer was a well-known doctor in Vienna. He had undertaken research on the physiology of respiration and also on the semicircular canals of the ears. Breuer became very important to Freud, who valued his wisdom, knowledge and understanding, and asked him for advice. As well as helping him make important decisions concerning his career, Breuer often took Freud on his rounds, and would later send him patients when he set up his own private practice. For years he regularly loaned Freud substantial sums of money when the latter was struggling financially. The pair would part ways in the 1890s over Freud's sexual theories.

ABOVE *Sigmund Exner (1846–1926), Austrian physiologist. He studied under Brücke in Vienna and Helmholtz in Heidelberg, then became an assistant at Brücke's Institute of Physiology. He succeeded Brücke as professor of physiology and director of the Institute in 1891.*

BELOW *Freud's sketch of the spinal ganglia of the* Petromyzon, *a primitive fish. His earliest scientific drawings are incredibly detailed, showing the cells he observed for hours under a microscope.*

best-known as Helmholtz's School of Medicine. Their principles for the study of organisms came to dominate the thinking of German physiologists and science teachers. The interplay of physical forces in a living organism was an important part of Brücke's physiology. He was also interested in evolutionary orientation: all organisms – plants, animals, and man – were part of one family, their differences being the result of developments. Darwin's theories of evolution were still being hotly debated, but researchers such as Brücke were working on the connections between organisms, the genetic relationships between species, and the similarities hiding behind the visual variety shown by different species.

Freud was put to work researching the histology of large and unidentified cells in the spinal cord of the primitive *Petromyzon* fish genus. He successfully identified the cells as spinal ganglion cells, showing

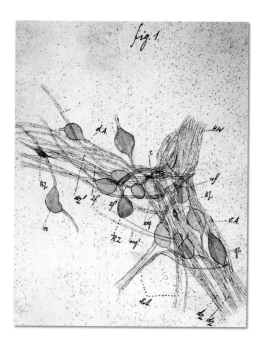

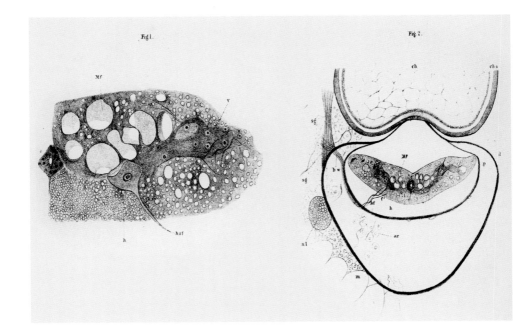

that there was a continuity between the nervous systems of lower animals and higher animals. This was a major discovery, as previously there was thought to be a sharp division between them. Freud's success was down to careful observation and interpretation, and his 86-page paper was advanced in its content and presentation.

He next researched the nerve cells of crayfish, studying them alive using a new and difficult microscopic technique. Although his work was solely involved with anatomy, there are hints in his papers that his research was conducted in the hope of beginning to understand nerve action. His ideas on the nerve cell and processes almost led him to an overall theory of the organization of the nervous system, but he did not dare to take the final step, and so he narrowly missed fame for a scientific discovery, and it was not for the last time. Neurone theory was instead first discussed by Heinrich von Waldeyer-Hartz (1836–1921) a few years later.

While studying, Freud also developed several technical innovations for his physiological studies. Brücke would have been astounded to see the

ABOVE *One of Freud's drawings for his 86-page paper on the spinal ganglion and spinal cord of the primitive* Petromyzon *fish genus. The level of detail betrays his almost obsessively close observation, and his love of laboratory work at this time.*

later development of Freud's career and ideas, but the principles upon which Freud constructed his psychological theories can in fact be recognized as those he acquired under Brücke's influence. The difficulties he encountered were in how to apply these principles to mental phenomena. While working in Brücke's laboratory, Freud met Joseph Breuer (1842–1925), who would also have a huge influence on the future of the young man.

Alongside research, Freud continued medical studies. He seems to have been unmoved by most of his distinguished and inspiring teachers. The only lectures that really interested him were those of Theodor Meynert (1833–1892), on psychiatry.

Freud's studies suffered a brief hiatus in 1879–1880, when he did his year's military service. This was not onerous as he lived at home and had no duties except to attend the hospital, but it was very boring so Freud undertook the translation of a book by British philosopher John Stuart Mill (1806–1873) into German.

Despite the varied interests Freud had pursued at Vienna University, he passed his final medical examinations in 1881 with the grade of "excellent." He alleged this was mainly the result of his photographic memory rather than sustained revision or preparation.

Freud returned to research under Brücke, working full-time at the Institute for 15 months and being promoted to demonstrator, which involved some teaching. He also did some research in a chemical laboratory, but saw no success in his investigations. Overall he termed 1882 as the least successful year of his professional life. If Freud had continued on as demonstrator, he could have aimed to eventually become professor of physiology in time. But the prospects for advancement any time soon were bleak, and he would leave the institute and research behind in mid-1882.

Although his father had allowed him free rein to choose his career regardless of material considerations, Brücke now strongly advised Freud to abandon a career solely in research, pointing out that because of his financial situation he needed to practice as a doctor to provide a living for himself. Freud had ignored the facts for as long as possible, concentrating on the laboratory work he loved, and avoiding the practice of medicine, for which he was not enthusiastic, but it could not continue. Freud knew Brücke was right about his finances, for although his needs were very modest, he was still dependent on his father's support. His father was not getting any younger, was not very well off, and had six other children. Freud had occasionally had to borrow from friends, but he paid it back as soon as possible. If he continued working under Brücke he would need to support himself by other means as well, and he certainly could not afford to marry and have a family. Until 1882, this last had not really been a consideration for the young Freud, but that year he met Martha Bernays (1861–1951) and fell in love.

TOP *Olmütz Town Hall. Freud had to serve for a month in the Landwehr during maneuvers at the small town of Olmütz in Moravia in 1886.*

ABOVE *Martha Bernays in 1884, two years after she met and became engaged to Freud.*

Finally accepting the truth of Brücke's wisdom, Freud began to set himself up for a career in private practice, beginning a three-year residency at the Vienna General Hospital. He entered the hospital as an aspirant and was later promoted to *Sekundararzt* (a junior or house physician), working in various departments. He lived and studied in the hospital for three years, acquiring knowledge of the various branches of medicine practiced there.

For the first two months, he worked in the surgical wards, which was physically tiring work. He then managed to obtain a position as aspirant in Carl Wilhelm Hermann Nothnagel's (1841–1905) internal medicine division, with help from Theodor Meynert, who recommended him to Nothnagel. Nothnagel expected dedication and long hours of study from his students, but was widely admired by them, and his patients. Freud respected Nothnagel, but was not interested in treating sick patients or studying their illnesses.

After six and a half months, Freud became Sekundararzt in Theodor Meynert's psychiatric clinic in May 1883. He felt Meynert was the greatest brain anatomist of his time, but had less respect for his abilities as a psychiatrist. Freud remained working for Meynert for five months, accruing psychiatric experience in both the male and female wards. He read voraciously, determined to get to grips with the theories.

Freud had continued to research the human central nervous system while training, and had written some papers on the medulla oblongata. Meynert, feeling perhaps that he was too old to keep up with the latest developments, suggested that Freud devote himself to the study of the anatomy of the brain, and offered to hand over his lecturing work to Freud. Freud declined the offer, choosing instead to specialize in nervous diseases, as there were few specialists in this area in Vienna, and he thought it would be good for his career and his pocket. He formed the plan of obtaining an appointment as a university lecturer on nervous diseases, then going to Paris to study under Jean-Martin Charcot (1825–1893).

Ernst Brücke (1819–1892)

Brücke was a German physician and physiologist, who accrued 143 publications to his name. He came to Vienna in 1848, and his institute in Vienna was an important part of the Helmholtz School of Medicine. It would also train many of the foremost physiologists of the next generation. Freud learned a great deal from Brücke's lectures, and from working for him. He would use the principles he acquired from Brücke to construct his psychoanalytic theories, even if Brücke himself would have been astounded to see how one of his favorite pupils had progressed from his intensively detailed studies in the laboratory.

On January 1, 1884, Freud moved to a department called *Nervenabteilung* – Nervous Diseases, though often there were no nerve cases there. The superintendent was Franz Scholz, who aimed to get rid of patients as quickly as he could. His priority was to keep down costs, so patients went hungry, were given the cheapest drugs, and the wards were dirty. There was no gas, so doctors made their rounds by the light of a lantern. That summer, while the superintendent was on holiday, a call for doctors to help with a cholera outbreak left Freud as the only doctor in the department. He enjoyed the position and pay of superintendent for six weeks, even though Scholz rebuked him on his return for spending too much.

Tensions continued between Freud and his superintendent, and in February 1885, Freud was told he was to be transferred to another department. Despite his pleas, he was moved to the Ophthalmological Department, until June when he moved to the Dermatological Department. He was there just a week before he took up a locum position at a private mental hospital outside Vienna.

Alongside his clinical work, Freud had continued to publish papers on diseases of the nervous system. In 1885, as he was shunted from department to department, he was successful in being appointed lecturer in neuropathology on the basis of his publications and following an oral examination and public lecture. The position was that of *Privatdocent*, a highly prized appointment, which was the first step to advancement in the university and greatly improved Freud's prospects for establishing a medical practice that would support a family. Also in 1885, Freud applied for a traveling bursary of 600 gulden, which came with a six-months leave of absence. Freud was determined to secure the grant, in order to get to Paris and Charcot. He canvassed hard to gain support in the vote, pulling in all the favors he could, and persuading anyone with influence to speak to other members of the faculty. The faculty met, and failed to decide who should have the grant, so it was referred to a subcommittee of three, each an advocate for one of the three applicants. Freud was in an agony of suspense, convinced he wouldn't get the money, but his advocate was Brücke, whose passionate intercession won him the funds. At the end of August 1885, Freud left the hospital and his general medical experience for good, bound for Paris.

BELOW *Vienna General Hospital, which Freud entered as an aspirant in October 1882, having decided he must acquire clinical experience in order to set up private practice.*

Freud in Paris

In October 1885, Freud received a bursary to enable him to travel to the Salpêtrière Hospital in Paris. In the late eighteenth century, it had been the largest hospital in the world, able to treat 10,000 patients, plus 300 prisoners, who were mainly prostitutes from the streets of Paris. The first humanitarian reforms in the treatment of the violently insane were trialled at the hospital by Philippe Pinel (1745–1826), when he moved there from Bicêtre in 1795. During Jean-Martin Charcot's time working and teaching at the Salpêtrière, the hospital became world-famous as a psychiatric centre. In 1882, he established a neurology clinic there, the first of its kind in Europe. Charcot is known as "the founder of modern neurology," describing multiple sclerosis and investigating

BELOW *The Salpêtrière Hospital in Paris. It was originally a gunpowder factory, then became a holding place for the poor, epileptics, criminally insane, and those with mental illnesses. Louis XIV had a hospital built on the site in the mid-sixteenth century, La Hospice de la Salpêtrière, which was expanded later that century.*

"*Paris means a new beginning to my life.*"

– SIGMUND FREUD

Parkinson's disease, but he is best known for his work on hysteria and hypnosis.

Until the seventeenth century, hysteria was considered to be an illness suffered by women, caused by disturbances of the uterus. In the nineteenth century, hysteria came to refer to sexual dysfunction. Charcot closely observed his patients to identify and characterize their disorders, and his investigations led to a new understanding of hysteria. Four stages of the major hysterical attack were identified, and the minor attacks related to this structure. He considered hysteria to be a neurological disorder, which some individuals were predisposed to develop owing to hereditary features.

Charcot investigated nervous illnesses that followed experiences of severe trauma. When studying hysterical paralysis appearing after stress, he managed to artificially replicate the paralyses. He introduced hypnosis to the hospital, getting patients to stare at a bright light until they became cataleptic. Closing the patient's eyes moved them to a state of lethargy, and pressure on top of their

ABOVE LEFT *Hysteria patients in 1887 at the Salpêtrière, collectively put into a hypnotic state by a sudden sound.*

ABOVE RIGHT *Jean-Martin Charcot (1825–1893). He became interested in the illnesses of the women in the Salpêtrière as a young doctor, and when he became a senior physician he permanently joined one of its departments for nervous diseases. He said that he was not a thinker, but a man who sees. Over countless hours, he observed the same symptoms and patterns among his patients, enabling him to identify "types."*

heads then created a state of somnambulism, during which they could receive communication from the hypnotist. He used this to successfully induce paralysis in hysterical patients, demonstrating how hysterical paralysis could result from psychological factors. These induced states were the same as spontaneous attacks. This meant that whatever caused hysteria, its symptoms could be treated and abolished by ideas alone. Charcot came to the conclusion that only hysterical patients could be

ABOVE *One of Charcot's doctors photographing a hysteria patient in 1883.*

ABOVE *A depiction of Charcot teaching on hysteria at the Salpêtrière. Blanche Wittman, the patient, was Charcot's most famous model, demonstrating the clinical patterns at his public lectures. She is held by one of Charcot's students, Joseph Babinski. Freud had a print of this painting above his consulting couch in later life.*

hypnotized, and his reputation and demonstrations gave hypnotism more status as a medical procedure. As well as proving that hysterical phenomena were real, he showed that hysteria also occurred in men.

Freud became an *élève* (student) at the Salpêtrière, one of a number of foreigners visiting the hospital at the time. He got to know Charcot better when he offered to translate Charcot's lectures into German, having heard the great man rant that he had lost touch with his previous translator, and needed someone to translate his new volume of lectures.

Freud was most impressed by Charcot's work on hysteria. As he watched the man at work, his prior interest in anatomy and research was abandoned, replaced by one in psychopathology and clinical work. Later in life, Freud admitted that although some of Charcot's ideas had been abandoned or disproved, the importance of his work could still not be disregarded. Charcot remained Freud's model of a scientist and physician, even after he no longer agreed with all Charcot's theories. When Charcot died suddenly in 1893 at the age of 68, Freud wrote an affectionate obituary, praising his qualities as a teacher and lecturer, and also his ability to inspire younger men, leading to the creation of a group of doctors and assistants willing to stay and work with him. His concluding sentences noted that not all of Charcot's ideas had remained intact and that although he had greatly overestimated the hereditary factor in causing nervous illness, this did not diminish Charcot's fame.

Before Freud left for Paris, he had been offered a position at the first public Institute for Children's Diseases in Vienna. This institute was being modernized, and Max Kassovitz had asked Freud to become director of a new neurological department. Prior to returning to Vienna he spent several weeks in Berlin, where he spent time at Adolf Baginsky's (1843–1918) clinic to learn about children's diseases.

On his return to Vienna, Freud presented what he had learnt from Charcot to the Society of Physicians (*Gesellschaft der Ärzte*) in Vienna, reading a paper on male hysteria in October 1886. His enthusiastic championing of Charcot's methods met with a cool reception. There were comments that he was presenting nothing new, and there was great scepticism regarding hypnosis. Freud was challenged by Theodor Meynert (see Chapter 3) to find cases of male hysteria in Vienna that were similar to those he had observed in Paris. Freud felt that he was blocked in this endeavor. Although he found suitable cases, the senior physicians of the department they were in refused to let him see or work with them. Eventually he found a man with "classical hysterical hemianaesthesia" outside the hospital, and presented it to the society. This was applauded, but then he felt his innovations were rejected.

Soon after this episode Freud was excluded from the laboratory of brain anatomy by Meynert, in late 1886. The two men's relationship had become strained after the publication of Freud's papers and it seems that it was this rather than a particular event which led to the exclusion. Freud then complained he had nowhere to lecture for a year, but this only

ABOVE *Hysteria patients, photographed having contorsions in 1876 (left) and exhibiting symptoms of a hysterical epilepsy attack, third period (right).*

ABOVE *While in Paris, Freud regularly took cocaine, using it as a stimulus, helping him manage his moods and relax. His mentor Charcot had also experimented with drugs in his day and this intricate drawing was done by Charcot under the influence of hashish. He would later show that hashish produced the same symptoms as hysteria.*

applied to his clinical demonstrations. He did lecture during this time on anatomy, to good-sized audiences. He described that after his exclusion from the laboratory he withdrew from the academic scene, and did not attend the societies any more.

The Cocaine Incident

In 1884, during his clinical studies at Vienna General Hospital, Freud had obtained some cocaine from Merck, a chemical firm, to study its possible uses in medicine. Cocaine is extracted from an alkaloid (chemical compound) found in the leaves of the coca plant. The leaves of the coca have been chewed for millennia by peoples of South America, who were well aware of its pain-numbing effects and uses as a stimulant and hunger-suppressant. The cocaine alkaloid was first isolated by a German chemist in 1855, and Western doctors were keen to exploit it. When Freud worked with it, it was still little known.

Eager to establish himself, and perhaps shorten the time until he could afford to marry his fiancée, Freud was always on the lookout for new methods or drugs that might make his name. Inspired by a paper by a German physician who had tried cocaine on Bavarian soldiers, Freud obtained samples in the hope that it would prove useful to his patients, though he did not know whether others might be undertaking similar research to himself. His first obstacle was paying for the drug, which cost far more than he expected, but he ordered a gram, hoping to be able to pay for it when the time came. Freud first tried it on himself, noting that it gave him a "normal euphoria." He studied its effect not only on himself, but on cases of heart disease and nervous exhaustion. He found it helped stomach disorders, and persistent coughing, and by regularly taking very small doses he treated his own depression and indigestion, with much success. He became more and more enthusiastic about the new drug, feeling it could help more of his patients in the future. He gave it to friends and colleagues for them to try, to

his sisters, and he even sent regular supplies to his fiancée Martha. His colleagues had mixed opinions of the drug, but that didn't sway Freud. He didn't think it was addictive because he himself felt no craving for it, regardless of how often he took it.

However, while undertaking study of this miracle drug, Freud had the opportunity to visit Martha (see Chapter 6), who had been living some distance away for the previous two years. He wound up his investigations quickly, and wrote up a paper on his findings. He was so desperate to see her that he also turned down other, lucrative work, and admitted to her in a letter that he would be taking "coca" on the journey to Wandsbek to curb his impatience.

His paper began with a lengthy history of the coca plant, and its uses, then covered his observations from his own consumption of the drug, listing the positive effects, and the lack of after-effects or cravings. He also discussed its action on the stomach, and the effect it had had on his patients, before concluding that the drug could be useful for those suffering neurasthenia (an ill-defined condition associated with emotional disturbance, and characterized by fatigue, headaches, and anxiety), indigestion, and during the withdrawal of morphine.

In the last paragraph, he noted that other uses for cocaine would soon be found. Later, he admitted that he had perhaps been lazy in not following up its potential use as an anaesthetic. Instead, he recommended to an ophthalmologist friend, Leopold Königstein (1850–1924), that he investigate the anaesthetic properties of cocaine for diseases of the eye. In the end, it was actually Karl Koller (1857–1944), another friend of Freud's, who first recognized the capabilities of cocaine to numb tissue as well as to ease pain. Koller began his medical career as a surgeon at the Vienna General Hospital, where he was a colleague of Freud. He investigated the use of cocaine in eye surgery by testing it on the eyes of

FAR LEFT *Freud in July 1884. Freud was invariably neat and correct, even in the 1880s when he and Martha were desperately saving for their marriage and he could afford very few clothes.*

LEFT *Martha Bernays. Freud blamed her for his missing out on fame by winding up his investigations into cocaine early because he was so desperate to visit her in 1884.*

animals. Soon after, he demonstrated its potential as a local anaesthetic. It was a medical breakthrough as eye surgery had previously been very difficult because of the way that the eye would react involuntarily to any interference. Königstein made a similar discovery, but just slightly too late, and had to cede the victory to Koller. Others soon followed up Koller's experiments, including the American William Halsted (1852–1922), who injected cocaine into nerves to produce local anaesthetic. Halsted then became addicted to cocaine and spent a long time overcoming the addiction. Cocaine was widely used as a local anaesthetic for many years, though it has since been replaced in Western medicine by synthetic local anaesthetics.

By passing on the information about cocaine rather than continuing his studies, Freud had narrowly missed out on scientific celebrity, though at the time he felt that the anaesthetic use of cocaine was peripheral, and that its value when taken internally was more important. It would be a long time before it would be obvious to him that Koller's use was the only one of import. In his autobiographical study, he notes that it was Martha's

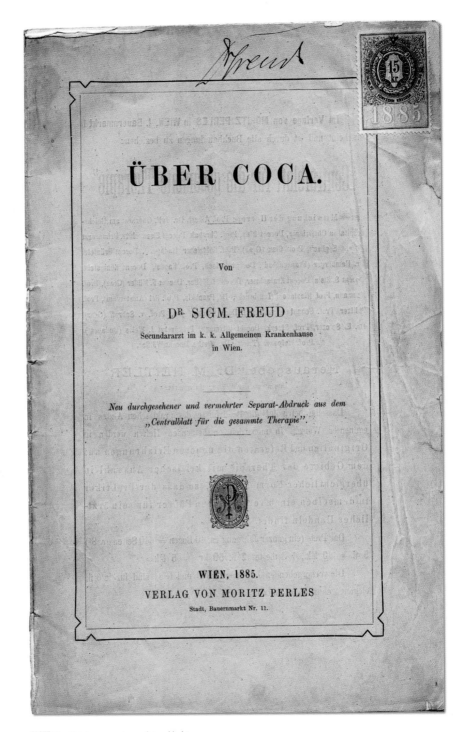

ÜBER COCA.

Von

Dr. SIGM. FREUD

Secundararzt im k. k. Allgemeinen Krankenhause
in Wien.

Neu durchgesehener und vermehrter Separat-Abdruck aus dem
„Centralblatt für die gesammte Therapie".

WIEN, 1885.

VERLAG VON MORITZ PERLES

Stadt, Bauernmarkt Nr. 11.

ABOVE *Freud's paper on cocaine, and signed by him.*

fault that he didn't become famous at the age of 28, but that he bore no grudge.

By the next year, 1885, the generous compliments Freud had received on his discovery and monograph were drying up, replaced instead with criticism of Freud's wholehearted recommendation of the drug to others. By 1886, cases of cocaine addiction were becoming widely reported, and he was attacked again in print, for unleashing "the third scourge of humanity." In 1887, Freud belatedly replied to the criticism levelled at him. He argued that no cases of cocaine addiction had been known when he undertook his studies except in the case of morphia addictions, indicating that addiction was related to something in the patient. Though correct, his argument didn't convince. He also argued that giving cocaine by subcutaneous injection was sometimes dangerous, and it was essential not to give injections of cocaine in any cases of internal or nervous maladies. This was a difficult line for him to argue, as he had previously advocated subcutaneous injections of cocaine.

The fallout of the cocaine incident also hit close to home on a human level for Freud. When public criticism of his actions was at their loudest, he ordered a large dose of cocaine for one of his patients, who died as a result. He was also reproached when another of his patients who, following his example, used cocaine and suffered considerable damage to her nose. Worst for Freud was the responsibility and guilt he felt for the death of a close friend. Ernst von Fleischl-Marxow and Freud had met in Ernst Brücke's laboratory (see Chapter 3) and had become very close friends. Fleischl-Marxow was an accomplished and charming man of many talents, and Freud was fond of him to the point of hero-worship. At the age of 25, his thumb had become infected following an accident when he was performing an autopsy, and it had to be amputated. Complications from this amputation caused him immense pain for years, and he became addicted to morphine and heroin. Freud prescribed him cocaine as a treatment for his addiction. Initially it seemed to work, and Fleischl-Marxow

was delighted. But instead of helping his friend, by his own later admission, Freud's cure actually hastened his death, and caused him more suffering. Fleischl-Marxow became a cocaine addict, taking very large quantities, around a full gram a day. Freud spent a lot of time with his dear friend, watching him suffer attacks of fainting with convulsions, severe insomnia, uncontrollable behavior, and eventually, owing to the large doses of cocaine he was consuming, delirium tremens. By mid-1885, Freud thought Fleischl-Marxow could only possibly live a few more months, but in fact he lived six more years, before finally dying a slow, painful death at the age of just 45.

ABOVE *Fleischl-Marxow (1846–1891) was an Austrian physiologist and physician. Freud, convinced that cocaine could treat his drug addictions, recommended that Fleischl-Marxow try it.*

Marriage and Family Life

In the autobiographical study that he was asked to write in 1924, Freud covers his engagement and marriage very concisely: "In the autumn of 1886 I settled down in Vienna as a physician, and married the girl who had been waiting for me in a distant city for more than four years." This summary little hints at the drama and stress of the four-year engagement, or the devotion of the 53-year marriage that followed, though both are fundamental to understanding more about Sigmund Freud.

In 1882, Freud was 26. An earnest young man, he was completely occupied with his work, and had little interest in women. His biographer, Ernest Jones (1879–1958), suggests that his lack of experience with women was also the result of considerable repression. All that would change in April 1882. One day Freud arrived home from work. He usually went straight to his room to resume his studies, but on this day he noted a happy young lady sitting at the table chatting with his family. It was 21-year-old Martha Bernays (1861–1951), who was visiting the Freud family, probably with her sister Minna. To his family's surprise, Freud joined them at the table.

After a few weeks, Freud realized how strongly he felt about Martha, and set out to win her heart. He sent a red rose accompanied by a motto, in Latin, Spanish, English, or German, every day. By early June, he felt fairly certain that the attraction was mutual, and he dared to send her a letter. Her response, on June 17, 1882, was to give him a ring that had belonged to her late father. It was too large for her to wear, so Freud wore it, and had a copy made for her to wear. The couple now considered themselves engaged, but it was a secret arrangement, with elaborate precautions

set up so they could write to each other without arousing their families' suspicions.

With no money to his name, Freud knew that he would have to make something of himself before he could marry Martha. Later that year he would make the decision to leave research behind and become a practicing doctor, but even so, it would be four long years before they finally married.

Martha's family came from Hamburg. Her grandfather, Isaac Bernays (1792–1849), had been chief rabbi of Hamburg, a learned and influential man. Martha's father, Berman (1826–1879), was Isaac's third son, and was a merchant. Unlike one of his two older brothers, who converted to Christianity, Berman remained true to his father's religious views for his whole life. When Martha was eight, Berman moved the family to Vienna, after becoming secretary to a Viennese economist, Lorenz von Stein (1815–1890). Berman died in the street from heart failure in December 1879, leaving his wife Emmeline (1830–1910), and three of the couple's seven children, Eli (1860–1923), Martha (1861–1951) and Minna (1865–1941) – the other four children pre-deceased him.

By the time she met Freud, Martha already had many admirers and suitors. A slim, petite, and intelligent woman with a charming manner, she had only just escaped engagement to a businessman many years her senior. Her brother Eli had dissuaded her from marrying at that time, as she was not really in love.

During their protracted engagement, several years of which were spent in separate cities, Freud sent Martha over 900 letters. Both wrote letters to the other daily, and a gap of two or three days required great explanation on the part of the neglectful writer. Some days they might write and send two or three letters. It is worth noting that these were not short letters, but four to 12 pages of close handwriting. The letters offer detailed accounts of daily events, much sharing of plans and hopes for the future, and are clearly extremely affectionate, showing a couple very much in love, though not always in agreement. There would be several storms for the couple before they reached marriage, some very serious. Freud wanted their relationship to be perfect, and expected Martha to side with him in everything, even against her own family. However, she did not give in to him easily, and on occasion rebuked him harshly.

Freud experienced several bouts of jealousy during their engagement, tormenting himself over her pre-existing friendships with two other men, even though both were totally innocent, at least on her part. After these issues were finally resolved, following much heartache and worry on both sides, he still had problems with Martha's family, particularly her brother and her mother.

He was annoyed by her devotion to her mother, and considered that she didn't stand up to her mother as he felt she should. Although she did write to Freud on the Sabbath, when writing was forbidden, Martha would write in the garden, and in pencil, rather than use pen and ink in her mother's presence. In June 1883, Emmeline decided to move her family back to Hamburg. She had hated leaving Hamburg, and never been completely happy in Vienna. By this time she knew of Freud's engagement to Martha, and her daughter Minna was engaged to Ignaz Schönberg, a close friend of Freud's. Despite the entreaties of her daughters, and

OPPOSITE *Martha Bernays was born on July 26, 1861, making her five years Freud's junior.*

ABOVE *Martha and Minna Bernays in 1874. Minna lived in Freud's household for over 40 years.*

ABOVE *Doctors at the Institute for Children's Diseases around 1895. Freud is seated on the far left. He worked there part-time for many years, making some valuable contributions to the field of child neurology.*

their fiancés, her mind was made up. Again, Freud felt that Martha did not argue strenuously enough to stay in Vienna, near him, and felt that she should always take his side, even against her mother. Martha refused, and he eventually admitted that he admired her more for not giving in to him. A couple of years later he wanted her to move away from her mother's home and influence, sure that they could find her a suitable position in Vienna. Martha suggested she stay with her brother Eli in Vienna

married in October 1883, and the couple lived in Vienna. Freud ended up feuding with Eli over various issues, and they did not speak for a number of years. A final storm in Freud and Martha's engagement was because of the largest hurdle to their happiness together – money – and involved Eli. They were counting every penny to be able to set up home together. Martha had entrusted part of her dowry to her brother, and he had invested it. When asked for it back, he did not have ready cash to pay immediately. Freud panicked and insisted Martha deal with her brother harshly. When she refused, he wrote a strongly worded letter to Eli himself, with the outcome that Eli repaid Martha the next day. Eli commented to Martha that he had no idea she needed the money so urgently, and that he was unimpressed with Freud's manner. Martha told Freud that she was unhappy with his behavior. Freud replied that Eli had been endangering their married happiness, and told her not to write again until she had broken off all relations with her brother. Her tact again won through, though she was utterly exhausted by the crisis.

During the engagement Freud's income came from several sources: his rather pitiful hospital allowance, abstracting for a medical periodical, seeing the occasional private patient, teaching pupils, and the translation of Charcot's book. He lived as cheaply as he could, sending every spare kreuzer to Martha for her to save for their future, and even sending her weekly accounts of his (frugal) daily spending. Martha was better off, living at home, but any money gifts from family were squirrelled away into the marriage fund. Freud struggled to buy any new clothes, asking Martha's advice before making any decisions, and on occasion had to borrow a coat from Ernst Fleischl-Marxow (see Chapter 5) to wear to visit a friend because his own coat was too threadbare. He regularly had to borrow from friends, and Breuer became one of his regular donors, for some time giving Freud a sum every month. Inevitably he ran up debt, and by mid-1885 he owed 1,500 gulden, a considerable sum. Help came from Joseph Paneth

until they found something suitable and commented that it would lessen the burden on her mother. Freud was furious, as she had thought of her mother first, rather than him, telling her she must renounce her family for his sake. She must have convinced him that he came first in her affections, for soon after he was on good terms with her.

Six months after Freud and Martha became secretly engaged, Martha's brother had proposed to Freud's eldest sister Anna. Eli and Anna (1858–1955)

(1857–90), who set aside 1,500 gulden to help Freud marry sooner, telling him he could spend the interest to visit Martha, and have the capital ready to use. In the end, Freud had to break into the capital while studying in Paris and Berlin. He most hated the fact that he could not send anything other than the smallest, and most infrequent, gifts to his fiancée, and visit her only rarely. He was also often worried about his own family, as his father was no longer earning, and his mother was ill. While he tried to help, often he could not spare any money to give them.

Eventually, although Freud had not yet made his fortune, they decided to make a date for the wedding, and a date was set for late 1886, after Freud had returned from Paris, and finally set himself up in private practice in Vienna. Joseph Breuer (see Chapter 7) recommended that he see lots of patients, and charge low fees, but was not optimistic of his chances in private practice. Freud worked at the Institute for Children's Diseases several times a week, and a friend asked him to help him with a journal he edited. In mid-April 1886, Freud set himself up in an apartment with two rooms and a hall, and began consultations. He announced he was open for business in the newspapers and medical journals, and sent cards to 200 doctors. Many of his first patients were referred by Breuer, and overall his first few months were more successful than he had expected, although he was not fully confident in his abilities as a general physician.

Freud was sent on army manoeuvres in the summer of 1886. This was another blow to the couple's plans, as it lost him a month's earnings and cost him in expenses. Before the wedding they still had to rent and furnish an apartment where they could live and Freud could work. The problem was solved by generous wedding gifts from two of Martha's relatives, and after his month in the army, Freud travelled to Wandsbek, where Martha and her family lived, for the long-awaited occasion.

Freud hated all ceremonies, particularly religious ones, and had consoled himself throughout their engagement with the fact that in Germany, they

could marry in a simple civil ceremony, avoiding a Jewish wedding. However it turned out that the civil ceremony would not be recognized in Austria, so they had to have a Jewish ceremony if they wanted to be recognized as married in Vienna, where they would live. To make it as easy as possible for Freud, Martha arranged for the Jewish ceremony to be on a weekday, and in her mother's home. So the day after the civil ceremony at the town hall, the couple had their wedding proper, with only eight guests and immediate family attending. Finally married, they honeymooned in the Baltic before travelling to Vienna, where they were warmly welcomed by Freud's friends.

The first phase of the marriage would be dominated by children, with Martha pregnant almost constantly for the first nine years. They had their first child, Mathilde, in 1887. Jean-Martin was born in 1889, and named after Charcot. Oliver, named after Oliver Cromwell, arrived in 1891. At this point the family needed more space, and so moved to Berggasse 19, Vienna. The year after they moved, a third son, Ernst, named after Ernst Brücke, was born. Freud then rented another flat, of three rooms, on the ground floor of the house to use for his private practice. The family

66 *I cannot think of any need in childhood as strong as the need for a father's protection.* **99**

– SIGMUND FREUD

OPPOSITE *A portrait of Freud and Martha to mark their long-awaited marriage, which took place on September 13, 1886.*

ABOVE *Freud and family in about 1898 in Vienna. From left back: Martin, Freud, Oliver, Martha, "Tante Minna," Sophie, Anna, and Ernst.*

ABOVE *Freud's waiting room at Berggasse 19, Vienna. Freud rented a ground-floor apartment in the same building in which he worked and saw patients for some 15 years before his sister vacated her flat opposite his on the same landing, and Freud adopted that as his offices.*

was completed by two more daughters, Sophie in 1893 and Anna in 1895.

Martha's sister Minna joined the household in late 1896, staying with the family until her death in 1941. Ignaz Schönberg had broken off his engagement to Minna in 1885, after being told that he would not recover from the pulmonary tuberculosis he was suffering from. He died in February 1886. Over the next decade Minna cared for her mother, also working as a lady's companion and children's tutor. She helped Martha with the household and children, hosting Freud's guests and students, assisting with his correspondence, and correcting his manuscripts. While Martha probably

did not keep up with all the details of her husband's research, it is clear that she did have knowledge of it, but running a household and her family left little time to pursue intellectual studies. Minna and Freud had a strong bond, and Minna probably knew more about his work than her sister. He commented that during his isolation in the 1890s (see Chapter 7), she was one of only two people to sympathize with his work.

There have been many rumors and stories about Freud's marriage and his work – that he was obsessed with sex and sexuality because his marriage was passionless, or that the end of the letter writing which characterized their engagement shows that it was a disappointing marriage, or even that he had an affair with his sister-in-law. He had several friendships with intellectual women during his life: as well as Minna he spent time with Emma Eckstein (1865–1924), Lou Kann, Lou Andreas-Salomé (1861–1937), Joan Riviere (1883–1962), and Marie

Bonaparte (1882–1962, see Chapters 16 and 17). His biographer, however, is clear on the fact that Martha was the only woman in Freud's love life. Even if the passion in their marriage waned relatively early, he was never interested in any other woman but his wife.

Freud was a family man. Life in the Freud household was happy and harmonious, with lots of jokes and teasing, and few quarrels between children or parents. His serious demeanor, particularly in later years, led some to assume he was not interested in his children. His biographer notes that his children were amazed to read in a book that Freud did not show them spontaneous affection, and was a severe patriarch. Instead, they remembered a man who shared their amusements, showed affection with hugs and devoted his spare time on holiday to them, teaching them to identify wild flowers and find mushrooms. Letters home to his children from his travels alone were written to amuse with their

descriptions of what he had seen and done, and seem full of affection. The only criticism Ernest Jones offered of Freud's parenting was that perhaps he was too lenient, letting his children grow up with far fewer restrictions than was normal at the time, but noted that it had benefited rather than harmed them! Freud was keen that his children did not worry about money as he had when young, and ensured that they always had everything they wanted, that they enjoyed holidays and travel and were given good clothes.

With six children under eight, the Freuds had their hands full, and Freud admitted to others that he did not work very hard. However, in 1891 he published his first book, *Aphasia*, considered the most valuable of his neurological writings. In this, Freud criticized a universally accepted doctrine of aphasia – a language disorder – and put forward his own views, including a new functional explanation for aphasia. While all his conclusions were later accepted, the book did not do well. He carried out other neurological investigations at the Kassowitz Institute, and by the mid-1890s was the leading authority on children's paralysis, but he now left neurology behind for new and uncharted waters.

ABOVE LEFT *From 1899, the Freud family spent many of their summers at a farmhouse near Berchtesgaden in Bavaria. This photo, taken that first summer, shows from left, Sophie, Ernst, Mathilde, Anna, Oliver, and Martin.*

ABOVE RIGHT *Freud's two youngest children: Sophie, his "Sunday child," and Anna, the baby of the family, photographed in 1901. Anna would be the only one to follow in her father's footsteps.*

The Beginnings of Psychoanalysis

The first few years that **Sigmund** Freud was in private practice he did not conduct much research, nor did he publish many papers. However, his work with his patients over these years was leading him onto a new path. Freud would devise a new therapeutic method that would open up previously unrecognized areas of research within which his discoveries would make his name.

The vast majority of the patients who came to Freud were suffering from neurotic illnesses. Initially, he had just two main therapeutic methods with which to treat them: electrotherapy and hypnosis, alongside baths and massages.

Electrotherapy was a common treatment for neurosis at the time, and Freud used it as described in the *Handbuch der Elektrotherapie* (*Textbook of Electrotherapy*) by Wilhelm Erb (1840–1921), regarded as one of the greatest names in German neuropathology. Freud used electrotherapy with his patients for 20 months, until he came to realize that it was actually ineffectual, despite being recommended by one of the leading experts in the field. He later commented that the experience helped him to lose his innocent faith in authority. He turned to hypnotic suggestion as a preferred method of treatment.

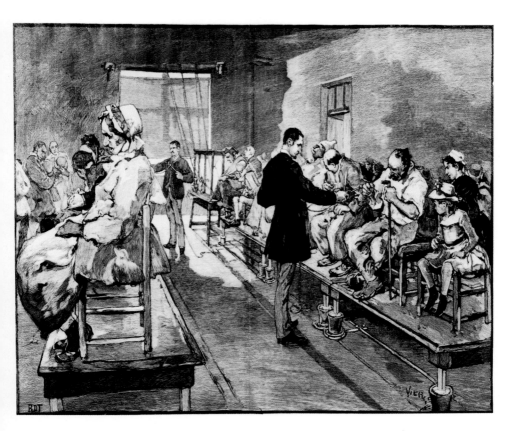

Freud had used hypnosis from the beginning of his private practice, having first seen it while a student, and of course having much experience of it at Charcot's clinic (see Chapter 4). A patient would be put into a hypnotic state, and the physician would make verbal suggestions to the patient – telling the patient to adopt a new mode of behavior or thinking that would help them overcome their symptoms. Freud would later bemoan the monotony of repeating suggestions, session after session, and eventually became dissatisfied with a method where the illness would be denied decisively in suggestion each session, but then had to be acknowledged to exist when otherwise speaking with the patient.

At this time there was a great debate over the efficacy, and safety, of hypnosis. While some German physicians took it seriously, others, including Theodor Meynert (see Chapters 3 and 4) regarded it as "hocus-pocus," or worse. Freud championed hypnotism, but he had two concerns with his treatment of choice: He couldn't hypnotize every patient, and he couldn't put patients into as deep a trance as he would have liked.

Charcot's ideas about hypnotism were challenged by Hippolyte Bernheim (1840–1919). Charcot felt that the phenomena produced by hypnosis replicated states seen in hysteric patients because there was a connection between the two, whereas Bernheim thought hypnosis was based on normal

ABOVE *Hypnotic session, 1887, by Sven Richard Bergh. Freud initially championed hypnotic treatment before becoming frustrated by limited results.*

psychological processes. Bernheim found no evidence for the three stages of hypnosis used by Charcot and found that hysteric patients were not especially susceptible to hypnotism, rather that most people could be hypnotized. Patients responded to hypnotic suggestions regardless of how deep their hypnotic state appeared to be.

after a short time. Bernheim tried treating her, but also failed. He told Freud that his greatest successes through suggestion were with his hospital patients, not his private patients. Even after his trip to Nancy, Freud still felt that hypnotism had its limitations, and began to consider what else he might offer.

Freud had known Joseph Breuer since his time in the Institute of Physiology. An adherent of the Helmholtz school, Breuer was an esteemed physician in Vienna and a well-regarded scientist who had undertaken notable research in his younger days. He was some years older than Freud, but the two became friends, sharing scientific interests. Their families spent time together, and Freud's eldest daughter was named after Breuer's wife.

Between late 1880 and June 1882, Breuer treated a young woman called Bertha Pappenheim (1859–1936), known in her case history as "Anna O." Bertha was a young, intelligent woman. After caring for her terminally ill father, she developed a complex illness over a period of time, suffering muscle contractions and paralysis, sleep disorders, an inability to eat, a nervous cough, and problems with her sight and speech; and instead of German, her native tongue, she spoke only English, even translating automatically into English when reading text in other languages. She seemed to have two personalities, one normal, the other similar to that of a naughty child. Between these two phases, she would spend some time each evening in a state of self-hypnosis. Breuer happened to visit during one of these trances, and she soon began to describe what had upset her that day, including her hallu-cinations. Relating it to Breuer seemed to bring her relief, and he began to visit regularly during this time each day so that she could talk to him. Some time later, she related how one of her symptoms began, and after doing so, she stopped suffering from it. Realizing what had happened, Bertha then talked through her other symptoms one by one, talking about how they came about, and in so doing resolving the trauma that had caused them. Eventually Breuer began to visit Bertha in the mornings as well, inducing a hypnotic trance during

In 1888, Freud translated Bernheim's seminal work and in the summer of 1889, he went to Nancy. He watched Bernheim's experiments and spent several weeks there perfecting his techniques. He took a hysteric female patient with him to Nancy. Although he had some success alleviating her symptoms through hypnotism, she always relapsed

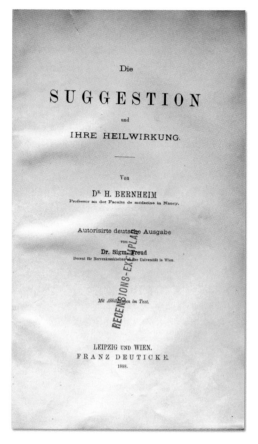

Die

SUGGESTION

und

IHRE HEILWIRKUNG.

Von

Dᴿ H. BERNHEIM

Professor an der Faculté de médecine in Nancy.

Autorisirte deutsche Ausgabe

von

Dr. Sigm. Freud

Docent für Nervenkrankheiten der Universität in Wien.

Mit Abbildungen im Text.

LEIPZIG UND WIEN.
FRANZ DEUTICKE.
1888.

Breuer first told Freud about the case soon after his treatment of Bertha ended in mid-1882. Freud was very interested in it, and would discuss the details with Breuer time and time again. While in Paris in 1885 he actually mentioned it to Charcot, but Charcot seemed uninterested.

Despite Charcot's lack of interest, Freud kept coming back to the details of the case, and as he started to consider how to treat his neurotic patients, it had an effect on the development of his methods. He was always intrigued by the origin of symptoms, and he began to try to use the hypnotic state to get at these origins using Breuer's cathartic method, as well as giving therapeutic suggestions. After his time with Bernheim, he worked at nothing else, and the earliest case in which he noted using the cathartic method was that of Frau Emmy von N. in 1889.

Freud still had trouble hypnotizing some of his patients, which made him think about methods to treat them that were not so dependent on the hypnotic state. He also began to see that the relationship between the patient and physician was important for the patient's recovery, and that hypnosis got in the way of this relationship, and in particular a certain aspect of it that he would come to call transference.

Over time, Freud began to use less hypnotic suggestion with his hysteria patients. Instead he began to move toward a listening cure, and his method evolved through the early 1890s. In 1892, he treated Elisabeth von R. She was not receptive to hypnotism, so he tried what he called a "concentration technique," which later became a method. It was the first time he had treated a patient without first inducing a hypnotic state. He would ask her to think of a particular symptom, and recall any memories that might be connected to its origin. When the patient stalled, he would press a hand to her head, telling her this would bring back more memories. He questioned and urged, feeling it necessary to help his patient along, but at one point Elisabeth reproached him for interrupting her, an occurrence which developed his method further.

which she could continue to talk. A significant part of his days was now taken up with this one patient, for over a year.

The treatment that developed was a new therapeutic method, one that she herself called "a talking cure." Instead of the patient being passive and hypnotized, Bertha talked actively to Breuer. Breuer called the method "catharsis."

By around 1895, Freud was treating his patients by encouraging them to say anything that occurred to him or her, rather than give an account of symptoms; this was the free-association method. The pressure on the patient's head had now been stopped, ending the hypnotic element of the treatment, though he would occasionally use hypnotism at certain stages of treatment with some patients for another year or so. The fundamental rule of free association was that the patient had to say everything that occurred to him or her, not censoring their words in any way, or leaving out anything that they felt unimportant. Freud felt that there must be something guiding the course of the patient's thoughts, and would patiently listen, not dismissing anything immediately.

Freud devised an arrangement of the physician's room to facilitate the process of free association. The patient reclined on a comfortable couch, while the listening analyst sat out of the patient's line of sight. Freud had learnt while in Paris with Charcot that patients reported different events when lying down. This has since been explained by modern neurology: when right-handed people are standing or sitting, the left hemisphere of the brain is used, which is responsible for logic and reason. When lying down, the brain switches to the right hemisphere, which is concerned with dreaming and associating rather than reasoning in memory.

Freud was keen that Breuer share the case of Anna O with the world. It took much persuasion on his part as Breuer didn't initially want to publish details of Anna O's case history in *Studien über Hysterie* (*Studies in Hysteria*) as he was embarrassed by the case. Bertha had become quite obsessed with him during the treatment. He had himself become engrossed in his patient after spending many hours with her, causing jealousy on his wife's part. In mid-1882, he decided he must bring the treatment to an end. Bertha seemed to accept this, but he was called back the same day to find her hysterical, proclaiming she was pregnant with Breuer's child, and even going into phantom labor. While she was calmed down by hypnosis, it is easy to see why

Breuer was not keen that her case, and therefore possibly its result, become public knowledge. Also, Bertha did not recover fully after her treatment by Breuer. She later became much worse, and spent time in a sanatorium, before reaching a stage where she was well during most of the day, and suffering hallucinations only toward the end of the day.

Freud only managed to get the full story out of Breuer after relating his own experience of a patient suddenly flinging her arms around him in affection, and his conviction that it was related to, and integral to, the treatment, rather than any actions on the part of the physician, or actual feelings on the part of the patient.

In 1893, the pair published a paper together in the *Neurologisches Centralblatt*. This was followed two years later by *Studies on Hysteria*. This book included the joint paper, five case histories, a theoretical essay from Breuer, and an essay by Freud. The first case history was that of Anna O, the second of Frau Emmy, the third of an English governess in Vienna, the fourth Elisabeth von R., and the final one being the case of a girl, Katharina, whom Freud had met just once, while on holiday in the Alps. This book is considered the beginnings of psychoanalysis.

Despite the importance the book is now seen to have in the development of psychoanalysis, it was not very well received at the time. While it had

some favorable reviews, others were very negative. A total of 800 copies were printed, and some 13 years later, nearly a quarter remained unsold.

Even before the book was first published, the co-authors were no longer as close as they had been, and soon there would be a permanent breakdown in their friendship due to Freud's new and sometimes disturbing ideas (see Chapter 10).

Freud felt that after his break with Breuer he was completely isolated professionally. He was no longer working at Meynert's laboratory, and he had no followers. He described himself as shunned in Vienna, and ignored abroad. He became increasingly reliant on one friend, Wilhelm Fliess (1858–1928). Fliess, who was two years younger than Freud, was a nose and throat specialist in Berlin. He was a charming and interesting man whom Freud's biographer described as being very fond of speculation and very confident in his ideas, refusing to acknowledge any criticism of them. Fliess and Freud met in 1887 after Joseph Breuer had met Fliess and suggested that he might like to attend some of Freud's lectures. Fliess had a background in physiological medicine like Breuer, but unlike Breuer, he had made sexual problems the center of his work, making him an ideal collaborator and mentor for Freud at this time. He formulated a number of rather idiosyncratic theories, including one that proposed a connection between the membranes of the nose and the genitals; several pertaining to cycles of life and theories based on numerology; and also the idea of innate bisexuality, which Freud incorporated into his theories.

Freud and Fliess soon became close friends. Freud would have named either of his youngest children Wilhelm, had they been boys. The pair had a similar background and overlapping interests. Their letters covered a vast array of topics and they met regularly to discuss their work.

In the 1890s, Freud was feeling alone in his scientific work and was suffering from illnesses, both physical and nervous. He needed someone to approve his work, back up his ideas, and give him confidence. He put Fliess in the position of mentor

and censor, sharing all his latest findings and ideas with him so the latter could pass judgement on them. In so doing, Freud seems to have credited his friend with the greater intellect and critical judgement to make him the mentor that he felt he needed at this time. He became quite dependent on Fliess for several years, and their rather intimate relationship caused jealousy, at least on the part of Fliess's wife. However, as with previous close relationships, this one too would be destroyed. In August 1900, they met to discuss their latest interests. Fliess said that Freud made an attack on him. The two never met again, though Freud tried to mend the friendship for a further two years.

OPPOSITE *Freud's couch, here shown in his last home in London, dates back to at least 1891. According to Martha Freud, it was given to him by a grateful patient.*

ABOVE *Wilhelm Fliess (1858–1928). The German nose and throat specialist met Freud in 1887 and the two became very close, writing and meeting regularly for over 15 years. Freud destroyed his correspondence from Fliess after their friendship ceased, but his letters to Fliess were purchased and preserved by Marie Bonaparte, offering a fascinating insight into Freud's state of mind in the 1890s.*

Dream Analysis

In ancient times, dreams were said to foretell the future. They could indicate favor or anger on the part of a higher power, or deliver a prophecy or instructions to the dreamer. Events or symbols in dreams were taken seriously, and could affect both personal and community decisions. Dreams and their interpretation appear in many ancient works, from the Babylonian *Epic of Gilgamesh* and the Bible to Greek tragedy, and an early literature about the interpretation of dreams developed in ancient Greece, including Aristotle's treatises on dreams and prophesying in dreams. Other societies through history have also put value on the interpretation of dreams, but by the nineteenth century, modern science saw dreams as unimportant, and it was unheard of for a serious scientist to choose to investigate the interpretation of dreams. In so doing, Freud was challenging the limits of scientific psychology. His work on the interpretation of dreams was his first major exploration of the general processes of repression, and the conscious and unconscious.

Freud had been interested in dreams since his youth, even then choosing to observe and record his own. Over time he compiled a private notebook

ABOVE *Aristotle (384–322 BC), the Greek philosopher, was one of many ancient authors to write about the genesis of dreams, and their meaning.*

Antiquities

Freud had a deep interest in antiquity from childhood and began to collect antiquities shortly after returning from Paris. Charcot also collected them. They appealed to him aesthetically, and were connected to his interest in archaeology, and in the origins of civilization. He would follow reports of archaeological digs and was particularly interested in the archaeologist Heinrich Schliemann, following his excavations at the site of ancient Troy and buying his account of his findings, *Ilios*. Freud would often describe analysis as peeling back layers, like archaeology. Freud acquired a huge collection of antiquities over his lifetime, many of them, like this statue of Imhotep, from ancient Egypt. He grew very attached to his collection, and was upset when he thought he would not be allowed to take it out of Austria when he emigrated to England in 1938.

of them, showing just how important he felt they were. His interest in the interpretation of dreams in the 1890s seems to stem from his work with patients, whose free association often led them into recounting dreams they had had, and also his experience of hallucinatory states in psychotics. Through his free-association method, he came to believe that the content of dreams came from the mind of the dreamer and had meaning, rather than being simply "the expression of a fragmentary activity of the brain, as the authorities have claimed." As early as 1895, Freud had formulated the crux of his theory of the interpretation of dreams.

As Freud set out in his book, he was interested in the significance of dreams, both their relation to other processes of the mind and their biological function, and also whether the content of dreams has meaning. Freud's completed theory about dreams, and method of using them, was based upon four main points.

First of all, the biological function of dreams is to protect sleep. They fend off both external and internal stimuli that could disturb the sleeper. External stimuli are given a new interpretation and formed into harmless situations, while internal stimuli are allowed to find satisfaction in dreams.

Second, dreams contain the residue of the previous day's thoughts and activities. These are woven into the dream, providing most of the imagery experienced. Freud labelled the imagery of the dream as the "manifest" content. Almost all dreams, however, also contain a wish, or an impulse, from the dreamer's unconscious, which is the "latent" content. Often the wish or impulse is something that would be repellent to the dreamer when he or she is awake. To Freud, these repressed wishes are infantile wishes, fantasies from childhood that have since been repressed because they are not acceptable in society.

Freud later acknowledged that some dreams didn't include the fulfilment of infantile wishes. This class of dreams was the repetitive dreams that someone might experience after a recent traumatic experience, re-enacting the trauma over and over.

Finally, this impulse is transformed by what Freud called "dream work," which used three main mechanisms – condensation, displacement, and dramatization – to evade the repression still exerted by the ego during sleep, and be fulfilled within the dream. Condensation is most familiar, where elements of several buildings or people may appear to the dreamer as one composite building or person.

ABOVE *Schloss Bellevue near Vienna. During his stay here in 1895 Freud managed to interpret a dream completely for the first time.*

ABOVE *Sigmund Freud in Vienna in 1897.*

Displacement causes a very trivial element of the dream to seem very important, perhaps repeating itself in the dreamer's mind after they wake, in order to distract from the underlying wish in the dream. Dramatization refers to how thoughts appear in the dream as imagery, mainly, but not always, visual imagery.

The dream is therefore a distorted translation of ideas and associations, almost all experienced by the dreamer in visual form. The level of distortion can vary, from a fairly intelligible dream through to the most bewildering and meaningless dream. In the simplest dreams, the manifest and latent content are the same. Freud classed children's dreams in this category, citing the example of a toddler talking about strawberries while asleep. The little girl had been denied strawberries that day because a previous glut of them had caused illness, and so in her dream was obviously enjoying a meal that included the forbidden fruit. Her dream was a direct fulfilment of her wish to eat

strawberries, without any disguise or distortion. The wishes in children's dreams are mainly connected directly to the events of the previous day, and adults often experience brief dreams of this infantile type, also connected to events of the previous day.

Dreams of the most confusing types can be analyzed to bring out the associations, and the "latent dream-thoughts" to express the meaning of the dream. Freud thought that the best way to interpret dreams was through free association, where the subject relaxes and talks about the contents of the dream, then lets his or her mind wander onto any related ideas or emotions. This then leads the dreamer, and analyst, away from the actual dream as experienced and onto the underlying content. However, when this elicited no helpful associations, Freud felt that it was possible to fall back on symbols that appeared so consistently in dreams that they could be considered to always have a similar meaning, regardless of the rest of the dream. Freud

OPPOSITE The Nightmare, *by Johann Heinrich Füssli, in 1781. Freud had an engraving of this painting in his study.*

ABOVE *Freud wrote significant sections of* The Interpretation of Dreams *during the summer of 1899 when he and his family stayed at this farmstead in Berchtesgaden.*

felt that these symbols were acquired by individual experience. These include things like a king and queen or emperor and empress representing the dreamer's parents, while rooms represented women, and genitals could be represented by many different things, including sharp weapons, or long objects like tree trunks.

In 1895, while on holiday at the Schloss Bellevue outside Vienna, Freud had a vivid dream, which became known as "Irma's Injection." He hadn't yet decided to write a book about dreams, but he recorded the dream when he awoke, and completed

a full analysis of it. It became the most celebrated of the dreams included in his book. The background to the dream was that Freud had been working with a young family friend, Irma. Her treatment had been only partly successful. While Freud was on holiday, Otto, an old friend, visited him after staying with Irma and her family, and commented to Freud that she was still not quite well. Later that day Freud wrote out her case history, in order to justify the treatment he had given her, and that night he had a dream.

Freud dreamed that he was in a large hall, welcoming guests to a party. Irma arrives, and he takes her to one side to reproach her for not taking his suggested treatment, telling her that it is her own fault she is in pain. She looks pale, puffy and unwell, and complains that pains in her throat, stomach, and abdomen are worse than he realizes. Freud worries that he has missed a physical illness, and gets her to open her mouth. He sees white patches and grey scabs in her throat. Several colleagues present, including Dr. M., examine her, with symptoms pointed out by Otto's relative and friend Leopold; the consensus is that she is suffering from an infection. They then become aware that when she had been feeling unwell earlier, Freud's friend Otto had injected Irma with propionic acid, probably delivered through a dirty syringe. The reaction to this is that injections of that sort should not be so thoughtlessly given.

Freud thought analysis of this dream was very useful because it had clearly been provoked by the events of the previous day, but the content itself was very confused. His examination of the associations within the dream fill many pages in his search for the latent wish hidden within. In his examination he noted that the person of Irma, her appearance and symptoms was a condensation: a combination of the real Irma, a friend of hers, and another patient of Freud's. Several details in the dream – the patches and scabs in Irma's throat and the repeat of his examination by his friend Dr. M. – seemed to point to occasions when Freud felt he had been insufficiently conscientious as a doctor. The comment about injections was an accusation of thoughtlessness against Otto, and the content of the injection was connected to a gift of noxious liquor which Otto had presented to Freud and his wife on his visit. The careful examination by Leopold also showed up Otto. The needle and comment about thoughtless injections was also associated in Freud's mind to his friend Ernst Fleischl-Marxow, to whom he had prescribed cocaine to treat his morphine addiction, and who had chosen to take the cocaine by injection (see Chapter 5).

Overall, the wish that Freud saw fulfilled in his dream was that he was not responsible for Irma's condition, but that Otto was (and that the other doctors present could also be blamed). Otto had annoyed Freud by his comments about Irma not being well the day before, and Freud's dream had played out a revenge against Otto in several different ways. There were several possible causes for Irma's illness in the dream, none of which could be considered the fault of Freud, so absolving him from any blame. Certain other themes played out in the dream which were all connected to Freud's concern for his own and other people's health and also his professional conscience. Freud thought these were in the dream because he felt Otto had been accusing him of not caring for Irma properly, and these details related to evidence for the fact that he was a conscientious doctor who cared about the health of others around him.

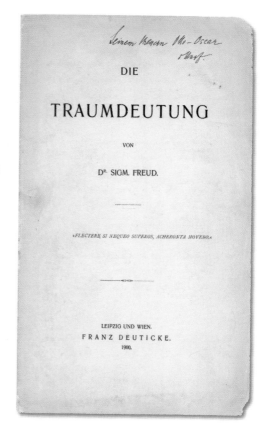

ABOVE *The title page of the first edition of Freud's most famous book* The Interpretation of Dreams, *which has been published in many editions since its first appearance in 1900.*

ABOVE *Anna Freud, Martha Freud, Freud, and Ernest Jones on the steps of the Schloss Bellevue in 1912. It was while staying here that Freud had his famous dream, Irma's Injection.*

The mechanisms that Freud found during the analysis of a dream were strikingly similar to those he had come across in analyzing psychoneurotic symptoms. He decided there was a difference between the nature of dreams and hysterical symptoms: Both are the disguised expression of fulfilled wishes, but while in dreams there is only the disguised wish, in symptoms there is a compromise between the repressed wish and the repressing agency.

Freud started considering writing a book on dreams in 1897, before he began self-analysis. The writing of his book, and his self-analysis were therefore carried out at the same time, and are closely linked. Many of the dreams dissected and discussed in the book were his own, making it a very personal, almost autobiographical book.

It took him two years to write, some sections being very difficult to write, and others coming surprisingly easily. The final section, on the psychology of dream processes, one of his most difficult and abstract texts, was written in just two weeks. In contrast, he found the review of the previous literature on the subject very tedious to write.

The book also introduced Freud's idea of the ego. He would later examine the ego, along with the id and super-ego in far more detail, but Freud reasoned that when the ego is concentrated on sleep, the repression it exercises when someone is awake is relaxed, allowing the impulses to push into consciousness, within the person's dream. There is still some repression present, which is why the impulse remains disguised. The dream is then a way for the impulse to be satisfied, a disguised fulfilment of repressed wishes. Freud felt that dreams were a "royal road to the unconscious", because thoughts are less censored during sleep, and so dreams can give clues to what is lurking in the unconscious. While useful to the analyst, this also offered an opportunity for the educated laymen, after reading Freud's book, to try and plumb the depths of their own unconscious minds.

Freud's opus, *Die Traumdetung* (The Interpretation of Dreams), was published in late 1899, although the date on the opening page is 1900. The 600 copies printed took eight years to sell. No scientific periodicals reviewed it, and few others mentioned it. It was essentially ignored. To illustrate the reaction in Vienna, Freud later recounted the example of an assistant at the psychiatric clinic who was writing a book to disprove Freud's theories without actually reading *The Interpretation of Dreams*, as his colleagues had told him it wasn't worth bothering with. The book wasn't completely ignored in the psychological periodicals, although the reviews were fairly scathing. Though exhausted by his work on his opus, Freud wrote a condensed version of the book for a wider popular readership.

Importantly, his theory of dreams applied to everyone, not just those with nervous illnesses. Freud declared in his book that dream work was only the first of a whole series of psychological processes which generated hysterical symptoms, phobias, obsessions and delusions to be discovered.

He also pointed out that many phenomena of everyday life, such as slips of the tongue, came from similar psychological processes. He would soon start to investigate these areas in more detail.

When the third revised edition was printed 30 years later, Freud wrote in the foreword, "Insight such as this falls to one's lot but once in a lifetime." He would regret that some of his ideas in the book were misunderstood and misrepresented, noting particularly that critics had attacked his ideas because of an assertion in the book that all dreams require a sexual interpretation, an assertion which occurs nowhere in *The Interpretation of Dreams*. In fact, half the dreams discussed in the book include wishes of ambition, or aggressive wishes against other people.

Over time, Freud realized that the importance of dream interpretation in therapy had to be downgraded. Interpretation of dreams couldn't be allowed to take over the treatment, as could sometimes happen when patients recounted multiple complex dreams. Instead, the overall aim of the treatment had to remain the analyst's main focus.

Despite the critical reviews after its first publication, *The Interpretation of Dreams* is widely considered to be Freud's most important contribution to psychology, and while dream interpretation has become less important in psychoanalysis as a therapy since Freud's time, he always saw it as a cornerstone to his theory.

Dora

In early 1900, 18-year-old Ida Bauer came to see Freud. Freud published her case history, using the name "Dora", in 1905, the first of his five major case histories. His decision to publish the details of her analysis without permission brought him strong criticism. Ida was suffering hysteria, the main symptom of which was aphonia, loss of voice. She recounted two dreams to Freud, who saw both as referring to her sexual life. Ida babysat the children of a married couple, Frau and Herr K. Frau K. was Ida's father's lover, and according to Ida, Herr K. had propositioned Ida since she was around 14. Freud considered her to be repressing desires for her father and feelings for both Herr and Frau K. After 11 weeks of therapy, she broke off her analysis with Freud, who acknowledged that the case history was the record of a failure. Despite being a "fragment" of a case, it incorporated dream work, Freud's theories on the unconscious, hysteria, and transference.

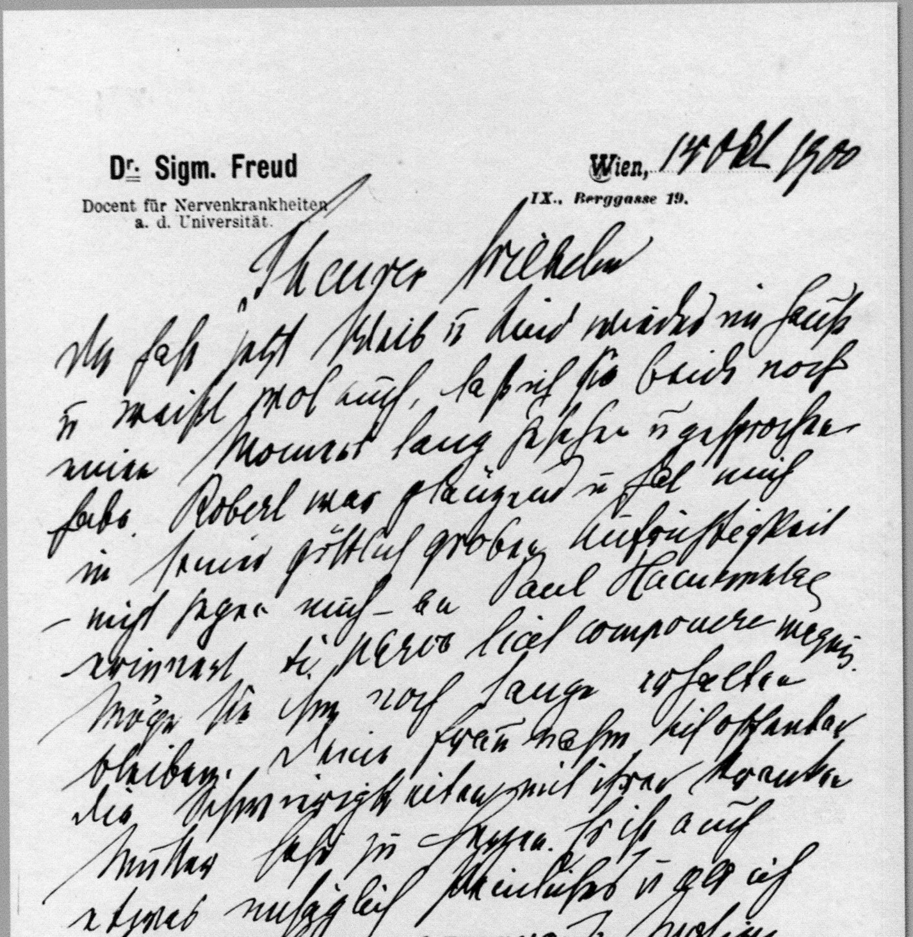

Dr. Sigm. Freud
Docent für Nervenkrankheiten
a. d. Universität.

Wien, 14 Okt. 1900

IX., Berggasse 19.

Theuer Wilhelm

Freud's letter to Wilhelm Fliess from October 14, 1900, in which he discusses the Dora case. (See Translations on page 170).

Repression of the Unconscious

Early in Freud's practice, he had wondered why patients had forgotten so many facts of their lives, but could be induced to remember them under treatment. Through experience he realized that patients were unwilling to disclose thoughts that were painful to them, and he concluded that these facts and thoughts had been forgotten precisely because they were painful. By making these disturbing thoughts conscious again, the patient could improve, but Freud realized too that there was something within the patient that fought to keep these thoughts unconscious. This he classed as "resistance." The effort required to overcome this resistance was related to the difficulty of the thoughts that had to be remembered. The information uncovered during the process of free association was not conscious before the treatment. It had been forgotten because it was distressing, alarming, or shameful to the patient. The disturbing thoughts had been repressed; memories were replaced with symptoms. This led to Freud's theory of repression, which became a cornerstone in the understanding of the neuroses. It was a discovery of which he was very proud, as nothing like it had ever been recognized.

Freud considered repression to proceed from the ego, and classed it as a primary mechanism of defence. He compared it with the flight instinct. As the ego cannot run from itself, the normal solution to disturbing thoughts, or "impulses" was for the "resistance" to struggle with it until the impulse was repressed and defeated. At a later date, the impulse might be rejected or condemned after judgement. However, in a patient suffering a neurosis, although the impulse was stopped from becoming conscious, it still wielded energy and was simply repressed, not defeated. The ego then continued to exert energy to keep the impulse repressed. The now-unconscious impulse would seek to discharge its energy, breaking through as a symptom in the patient.

Initially, Freud felt he had to force the patient to overcome repression in the mind, but this caused strain to both analyst and patient, which helped prompt the development into free association.

His new therapeutic method aimed to encourage his patients to talk about their symptoms, eventually tracing them back to their origins. Although at times their wandering thoughts might seem unconnected or random, Freud was sure there must be something guiding and determining their direction. Once he had realized that certain impulses and ideas were being repressed, he concluded that the wandering thoughts being voiced were an expression of the resistance. The patient's resistance would first be expressed through critical objections, which is why Freud insisted that the patient report absolutely everything that occurred to him or her.

If there was only slight resistance, the analyst could work out from the patient's allusions during free association what the unconscious material was;

RIGHT *The English physician and writer Havelock Ellis (1859–1939). His book* Studies In the Psychology of Sex *(1927) was the first book to treat the subject without guilt.*

if resistance was stronger, the analyst had to try and recognize its character from the associations that the patient mentioned. Because the patient led the analysis, nothing could be introduced by the expectations of the analyst, and no factor would be overlooked. If the patient recounted dreams, this would give the analyst another way of seeing unconscious, repressed thoughts.

Freud's aim was to uncover repressions in his patients, and replace them by acts of judgement. This therapy had been developed further than Joseph Breuer's cathartic method (see Chapter 7), and in 1896, Freud used the phrase psychoanalysis for the first time, in a paper published in French and German.

Freud distinguished between stages of repression in a later paper, noting that repression is individual and mobile. Repression was a constant battle to keep impulses unconscious. The mobility of repression is shown by its relaxation during sleep.

Freud was interested in repression of the unconscious not only in those suffering mental illness, but in the functioning of the conscious and unconscious in the mind more generally. In 1905, he wrote an entire book on jokes and their relation to the unconscious. In it, he argued that in jokes, unconscious thoughts that are usually repressed are allowed to be expressed. Jokes use mechanisms similar to dream work, such as condensation and displacement (see Chapter 8), but are intended for an audience. Jokes are funny because they express repressed thoughts – often impulses relating to sex and aggression – topics which often cannot be expressed openly.

Later in his career, Freud would discuss the importance of another mechanism of the unconscious in therapy. He recognized that analysis created an intense emotional relationship between the patient and analyst, which he would call "transference." This was not a phenomenon of analysis, but a universal phenomenon of the human mind that was simply uncovered during analysis, where the patient's behavior toward the analyst was shaped by their unconscious. The patient might feel anything from passionate love to bitter hatred toward the analyst, related to previous emotional relationships experienced during the repressed period of childhood. It was transference that caused Anna O to profess love for Breuer, causing him crippling shame about the case (see Chapter 7).

Initially, Freud felt that transference was an obstacle to treatment, but in fact the analysis of the transference proved important to the treatment. If positive, it can replace the patient's desire to be

cured, and can help the analysis, but can also lead to a false "transference cure." Negative feelings toward the analyst can instead be the tool of the resistance, stopping the patient from being able to associate. Exploration of transference can reveal unresolved issues in previous relationships, which the patient can then explore and overcome. In this way, transference becomes the best instrument of the analysis.

The emphasis in psychoanalytic treatment was slowly changing to the opening up of communication between analyst and patient through the analysis of the transference relationship. The transference has to be discussed at the appropriate time in the treatment, and has to be dissolved before treatment ends.

The study of repression led Freud to consider the unconscious more fully. He was not the first to study the unconscious, but he was the first to devise methods to systematically study it. He asserted that while repressions are unconscious, they are by no means all that is unconscious. Psychoanalysis regards everything mental as unconscious in the first instance. People are aware of things that have then been transformed into consciousness.

His theory of the unconscious evolved to include three levels of consciousness. The preconscious comprises information that is available, and is capable of becoming conscious but not immediately present in the conscious. Freud then developed his topographical scheme of mental acts further, to see the unconscious as comprising three types: the descriptive unconscious, dynamic unconscious and system unconscious. The descriptive unconscious covers all those features of mental life of which we are not subjectively aware, such as the everyday actions and behaviours that are not controlled consciously. To this Freud added the idea of a dynamic unconscious. The dynamic unconscious constantly affects our behavior. Its influence is shown up through slips of the tongue or attributes like courage. Finally, Freud identified the system unconscious. when mental processes are repressed, they become organized by principles different from those of the conscious mind. This scheme of unconscious, conscious and preconscious, and the various types of the unconscious would later be superseded by Freud's model of the ego, super-ego, and id (see Chapter 14).

Freud loved jokes, and often used them to illustrate a point. He started collecting jokes at least by the mid-1890s, and had collections of both Jewish jokes and war jokes, of which this manuscript is part. As with slips of the tongue, he spent time analyzing jokes, which he felt were told to satisfy unconscious desires.

g) liebe Eltern Schreibt ein in das zwischen
armee jemanden her nach hause. Es geht
mir sehr gut auch Ihre schließe ein paar
markten zurück So laßt wohl hoffe ich
zu Roschhaschono zu hause zu sein

h) Fürs Schütz - ein Kuß
Jedes Roß - ein Franzos
Jeder Tritt - ein Britt
Jeder Stoß - ein Japs

i) Poincaré - Schweinekarré

j) Belgien mitt zwischen England u. Deutschland gelaust. England bekannt Van-
dung und Deutschland das auch.

k) Der treibend tröstet sich meines preissen
und meinen Magadvine

Freud's Theories on Sexuality

Sigmund Freud and Joseph Breuer's collaboration, *Studies on Hysteria*, did not really look into the causes of hysteria, but Freud had become increasingly convinced that the emotional issue which underlaid hysteria was of a sexual nature, either a current sexual conflict or a past experience.

His patients' search for the origin of their symptoms through therapy often led right back to their early years. Freud felt that the experiences of early childhood, whether consciously remembered or not, left traces on a person's development, and in particular laid the disposition for later nervous illnesses. As he listened to his patients talk, Freud became convinced that these early experiences underlying hysteria were of a sexual nature. From his patients' reporting of their early memories he concluded that they had been seduced, or sexually abused, as children. His hypothesis that the roots of neurosis lay in sexual seduction in childhood was strengthened by several of his cases where the abuse had continued until the subject was older.

This discovery was not welcomed by the majority, who were upset by the idea of childhood having a sexual element. His good friend Breuer was horrified by Freud's seduction theory, and although he initially tried to defend Freud and his theories in public, he just couldn't agree with Freud's ideas, and the friendship ended as a consequence.

Undeterred, Freud continued to work on his theories, but a few years later, he realized he was wrong. Many of the "seductions" his patients had

ABOVE *Hamlet, as played by Otto Sommerstorff in Berlin in 1902. Freud's brief psychoanalysis of Hamlet concluded that Hamlet's actions were influenced by his repressed childhood wishes to kill his father and take his father's place with his mother. In his writings, Freud would note how the Oedipus complex was expressed in writing and drama, and several of his followers pursued these lines of investigation.*

The Oedipus Myth

In Greek mythology, Oedipus was the son of King Laius and Queen Jocasta of Thebes. Before his birth it was prophesized that he would kill his father and marry his mother, so his father abandoned him in the wild as a baby. He was rescued and brought up in Corinth. When grown, he heard the prophecy, so attempted to avoid the fate by leaving home, choosing to go to Thebes. On the road, he met Laius, they argued, and Oedipus killed him in self-defence. Further along the road he met a sphinx, which asked all travellers to Thebes a riddle, and killed and ate those who could not answer. Oedipus answered the riddle correctly, and the sphinx killed itself, freeing Thebes. The grateful Thebans made Oedipus king, and gave him the hand of Jocasta in marriage. Many years later, when the truth finally emerged, Jocasta killed herself, and Oedipus gouged his own eyes out. Freud used the name Oedipus for the complex he proposed was experienced in early childhood, where the child loves the parent of the opposite sex and hates the parent of the same sex. On the left is an early fourth-century BC Athenian water vessel shaped as a sphinx from Freud's collection.

recounted had never taken place. He had had growing doubts about the theory as it appeared that if it were true, then according to his patients a large proportion of fathers had abused their children, and the hysterical symptoms shown by his siblings meant that even his own father must have abused his children. The realization that all recalled memories may not be true was connected to his own self-analysis, undertaken in the summer of 1897. This realization that these stories were not real shook him, as he felt his therapeutic method was correct, and that sexual issues were central to nervous illness. Also, he didn't feel he had forced these "recollections" upon his patients.

It was a turning point in his scientific career. Was his psychological method flawed? Were his ideas ridiculous? In September 1897, he wrote to his friend Wilhelm Fliess (see Chapter 7), admitting that he no longer believed his seduction theory. But he was not downhearted. While abandoning his theory was a

great wrench, he then came to the realization that if accounts of abuse were not necessarily true, the fact that they were false memories was crucial. These imagined stories, these fantasies of his patients, were real to them, and having real effects. So he now knew that in finding the causes of neurosis, psychical reality was as important as actual reality.

The development of his theory was important for Freud, but very controversial. Critics argued that he was denying patients' experiences of abuse, and that he had only changed his theory to avoid reporting widespread sexual abuse of children. In fact, Freud never denied the reality of abuse.

It was the assertion that children had sexual feelings that really shocked his contemporaries. Freud was interested to see what role the sexual factor played in other forms of neurotic trouble, grouped under the term neurasthenia. By 1893, he had concluded that all neurasthenics had disturbed sexual function, the rationale being that sexual

LEFT *In 1907, Freud analyzed Gradiva, a novella by Wilhelm Jensen, as his research interests expanded to take in almost all cultural phenomena. Freud described his paper: "I was able to show from a short story ... called Gradiva ..., that invented dreams can be interpreted in the same way as real ones and that the unconscious mechanisms familiar to us in the 'dream work' are thus also operative in the processes of imaginative writing." This reproduction of the Gradiva hung next to Freud's couch.*

OPPOSITE *Bookplate created for Freud by Bertold Löffler in around 1901, showing Oedipus and a sphinx. The Greek is from Oedipus Rex, and roughly translates as, "He who knew the famous riddles and was the mightiest man."*

tension created libido (sexual hunger), but when libido is checked, and unfulfilled for any reason, the tension is transformed into anxiety. He categorized two forms of neurasthenia – anxiety neurosis and neurasthenia – dependent on how the patient's libido had been thwarted. The anxiety caused is a physical effect, and so could not be treated by analysis; instead, causing the patient to resume normal sexual activity would improve their health.

Over the next few years Freud would leave behind the idea of children as innocent objects of incestuous desire, and create a theory of infantile sexuality where children possessed sexual feelings that were liable to repression, elaboration, and distortion throughout development.

According to Freud, children go through phases in sexuality right from birth. The first stages concern a narcissistic, or self-love. The phases of psycho-sexual development in infancy are all rooted in the physiological development of the baby and his or her relationship with the world, as they become less dependent on parents.

Later in infancy, children develop a desire for their parent of the opposite sex, and hatred of the parent of the same sex. This is Freud's Oedipus complex, which he introduced in *The Interpretation of Dreams*, and developed right through to his last years.

The Oedipus complex has to be repressed in order for the child to continue to develop normally. Freud thought that girls and boys resolved the Oedipus complex differently as a result of boys' "castration anxiety," caused by Oedipal rivalry with the father, and girls' "penis envy."

Freud increasingly felt that the Oedipus complex was the nucleus of the neurosis, the climax of infantile sexual life, and the point from which all later developments proceeded. He felt that if the Oedipus complex was not successfully resolved, then the results could be neurosis, paedophilia, or homosexuality. After the climax of the resolution of the Oedipus complex, a child's impulses are repressed until puberty. At puberty the impulses and urges of a child's early life, including the Oedipus complex, reassert themselves, and there is a struggle between

these urges, and the inhibitions acquired between the ages of five and puberty. In *The Interpretation of Dreams*, Freud commented on how the Oedipus complex appeared in writing and drama, including Shakespeare's *Hamlet*. His idea would be expanded by others including Ernest Jones, who wrote a study called *Hamlet and Oedipus*.

Overall, Freud developed several general theories on sexuality. He did not consider sexuality as necessarily connected to the genitals. Instead he saw it as being a pleasure-seeking function, with reproduction as a second goal. Looking at sexuality in this way enabled him – as he put it – to consider the sexual activities of children and adults with sexual "perversions" in the same scope as those of normal adults. He also felt that all affectionate

Otto Rank (1884–1939)

From a poor family, Otto Rank attended trade school, writing and reading widely at night. He wrote an essay explaining the artist and art through psychoanalysis after reading *The Interpretation of Dreams*. When Freud read it, he appointed Rank as secretary of the Psychological Wednesday Society. Rank had become one of Freud's earliest and closest followers, aged just 21. Freud advised him not to go to medical school, but instead study at university, and supported him through his Ph.D. studies. He was highly intelligent, and developed a flair for analyzing dreams, myths, and legends. In 1912 he published *Das Inzest-Motiv in Dichtung und Sage (The Incest Motif in Poetry and Saga)*, discussing how the Oedipus complex provided themes in literature and myth. He was the most prolific psychoanalytic author after Freud himself. Ernest Jones said that the First World War changed his personality considerably, and Rank began to move away from traditional psychoanalysis in the 1920s. He finally broke with Freud in 1926.

OPPOSITE *Painting of the* Wolf Dream *by Sergei Pankejeff. Pankejeff was treated by Freud between 1910 and 1914, and Freud published his case history in 1918. It has been called the most elaborate and important of Freud's case histories, bringing together the main aspects of catharsis, the unconscious, sexuality, and dream analysis. In it, Freud focused on the Wolf Man's childhood neurosis, and the complicated evolution of his sexuality. The patient's dream of being terrified by wolves in a tree outside his bedroom window – analyzed by Freud to be a result of Pankejeff seeing a "primal scene," his parents having sex as a very young child – was central to the understanding of his neurosis.*

RIGHT *Freud's Sexualschema diagram, a "schematic diagram" for sexuality which he seems to have formulated in early 1895, and which he sent to Wilhelm Fliess with a manuscript, "Melancholia," for him to comment on. He also created a more complex schematic for anxiety neurosis and neurasthenia.*

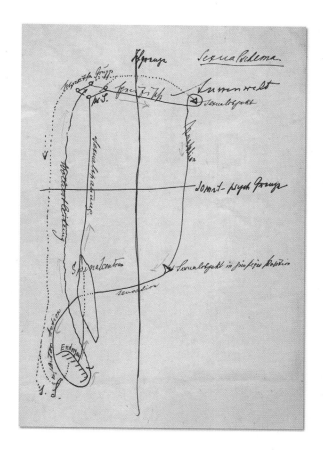

and friendly impulses, often described as love, were sexual impulses. Initially solely sexual, these impulses were inhibited, or sublimated, in some way.

After Freud wrote *The Interpretation of Dreams*, he concentrated on theories of sexuality, writing *Three Essays on the Theory of Sexuality* (published 1905), which he wrote alongside his book on jokes. *Three Essays* is probably the second most important book that Freud wrote, advancing his theory of sexuality. It was initially a small book of around 80 pages. He continued to enlarge on it, publishing six editions, the last of which was 40 pages longer than the first. The book brought together all Freud had learnt from his patients about the development of the sexual impulse from childhood.

The first of the three essays discussed the "sexual aberrations" – deviations from what was considered normal in the sexual instinct, including homosexuality, bisexuality, paedophilia, fetishism, sadism, and masochism. The second essay focused on infantile sexuality. It discussed the manifestations of infantile sexuality (which even included thumb sucking), infantile masturbation, and the stages of sexual development (this section was added in 1915). The final essay covered the transformations of puberty.

The book, particularly the discussion of infant sexuality, and the assertion that babies are born with sexual urges, caused horror, and Freud was much attacked and criticized. The reaction went on as he continued to work on new editions of the book and elaborate his theories on sexuality, over the next two decades.

Doctor Becomes Patient

The 1890s were an important period for Freud. In his "splendid isolation" he set off on his own path, formulating the main concepts of his psychoanalytic theory, under the critical eyes of Vienna. At the same time he was also a father struggling to support a young and growing family, his youngest daughter Anna being born in 1895. The following year his father, Jakob Freud, died. The decade also saw his intense and intimate relationship with Wilhelm Fliess (see Chapter 7) blossom and

then wither. Given the strain he must have been under, it is hardly surprising that Freud struggled with his own internal conflicts during his early 40s.

While Freud did not suffer serious illness until his 60s, he seems to have been constantly beset by minor health issues. He often mentioned his stomach problems in letters; these were diagnosed as many different ailments over time. Freud's biographer Ernest Jones suggests that they may have been at least in part psychosomatic. He was afflicted by

LEFT *Max Pollack's sketch of Freud writing at his desk in 1913. It is probably the first image to show Freud with his beloved antiquities.*

severe migraines throughout his life, and had severe nasal catarrh and sinus complications. During the 1890s Fliess operated on him twice for nasal problems, and also prescribed him cocaine. Freud also suffered rheumatic pains in his arms and right hand, a plague for a man who loved to write so much.

In 1894, he had some heart problems, having suffered heart arrhythmia since having influenza five years previously. He endured two or three attacks a day where his heart raced, or was irregular, and pain radiated down his arm. The heart problems were attributed to nicotine poisoning and he was told to stop smoking, but he preferred to continue, and risk shortening his life. The irregular action of his heart was controlled by medication, and he then agreed to reduce his smoking, from around 20 cigars a day to one a week. He abstained completely for over a year before he could stand it no longer, and began smoking again. Jones considers this heart trouble to be an aspect of his psychoneurosis rather than myocarditis, as he was otherwise a fit and healthy man who thought nothing of striding up mountains.

It isn't clear when Freud began to experience psychological illness. However, as a young man he suffered from what he termed "neurasthenia" (see Chapter 10), which continued until some time after his marriage. It caused intestinal problems, exhaustion and moodiness, and left him bereft of enjoyment for life. At the time he put it down to his lifestyle, which was after all very stressful. He always felt better when he spent time with Martha, and was convinced during their engagement that he would be absolutely fine once they were eventually married. However, this was not the case, and in fact his problems would worsen during the first years of their marriage.

During the 1890s, Freud suffered from what was quite a serious psychoneurosis. It may be hard to fit this with the energetic physician, scientist, and father of the period, and indeed he continued to work, care for his family, and function so successfully that most people who met him at this time would have had no idea of his internal sufferings. Apart from anything else, he did not stop working at any point because he couldn't afford to. His patients, and earnings, varied tremendously month to month, and he was supporting a dozen people. While his ambitions were still to discover rather than advance socially or professionally, he acknowledged that Vienna was a snobbish society where patients consulted the most exalted doctor they could afford, and such reputations were based solely upon the title held by the doctor. The richest would consult only professors so this was the only reason that Freud had any interest in obtaining the title of professor. During the 1890s, he was passed over repeatedly for this role, despite the support of friends including Hermann Nothnagel (see Chapter 3), and his reputation as a neurologist, both of which were overshadowed by the anti-Semitic attitude in official quarters in Vienna, and not helped by Freud's work on sexuality. Eventually he did become professor, but only because one of his patients struck a bargain with the necessary authorities. Freud was obviously

ABOVE *Freud's father Jakob in 1890 when he was 75 years old.*

ABOVE *Freud with his mother and sisters at his father's grave in 1897.*

pleased as his practice began to improve, though he felt that, knowing Vienna as he did, he should have realized earlier what he needed to do to achieve success.

Freud acknowledged the great suffering that his neurosis caused him. While he had few physical symptoms, he underwent extreme changes of mood, from elation and extreme self-confidence to severe depression and doubt, when he could not focus or work. He also had attacks of a dread of dying, and anxiety about travelling by rail. In fact, throughout his life Freud would be much preoccupied by thoughts of death. It was mentioned often in his letters, and he spoke of it to friends and colleagues. When he was a young man it was fear of it that preoccupied him. Later, when fighting oral cancer (see Chapter 13), he would talk of a wish for death, and release, though his feelings on this were ambivalent right until the very last days of his life. In

the 1890s, he was quite convinced that he would not live a long life, partly because Wilhelm Fliess had predicted he would die at the age of 51 (which he turned in 1907), and was worried that he wouldn't finish his new psychology in time.

The one person in whom he fully confided about his neurosis was Fliess. Ernest Jones felt that this showed there was a connection between Freud's neurosis and his relationship with, and dependence on, Fliess. He notes that Freud's neurosis, and his dependence, were at their worst in the last years of the decade. Jones also saw a connection between the fact that Freud's neurosis coincided with the period when he did his most original work: "The neurotic symptoms must have been one of the ways in which the unconscious material was indirectly trying to emerge, and without this pressure it is doubtful whether Freud would have made the progress he did." His conclusion was that Freud's exploration of the unconscious, and his dependence on Fliess, had some inner meaning for Freud, which resulted in his neurosis.

As well as his relationship with Fliess and his work on the unconscious, another major event of this decade affected Freud's state of mind – the death of his father in October 1896. Jakob Freud died after several months of illness, at the age of 81. Freud wrote to Fliess in November: "The death of the old man has affected me profoundly. I valued him highly, understood him very well, and … he meant a great deal to me." He classed the death of the father as the "most important event, the most poignant loss, of a man's life." His neurosis was at its worse in the years after his father died.

It was also after his father's death that he began his own self-analysis, the first time that such a thing had ever been done. In later years, Freud would train new analysts by making them patients and putting them through analysis. In essence he was doing that to himself in the late 1890s. Freud had previously done some analysis of his own dreams, which gave him the conscious idea to complete his own self-analysis, and the process continued as he worked on *The Interpretation of Dreams* (see Chapter 8).

In April 1897 he wrote to Fliess, "My recovery can only come about through work in the unconscious. I cannot manage with conscious efforts alone." After this, Freud suffered a period of apathy, when he was unable to write and he began to realize that the way ahead was through a personal psychoanalysis. In early July he mentioned to Fliess in a letter that there were resistances in the depths of his neurosis that were connected to Fliess.

In the summer of 1897, Freud began the self-analysis of his own unconscious. The examination of his dreams in particular became a preoccupation, interpreted through the method of free association, but he also collected up his memories, his slips of the tongue, instances of forgetfulness, and other minor events of his life to use as clues in his search. His neuroses actually worsened, or at least became more manifest, for several years before he began to feel better. His letters to Fliess over this period carefully record his progress, providing Freud with a way to create the dialogue present in normal analysis. In October 1897 he wrote, "My self-analysis is in fact the most essential thing I have at present and it promises to become of the greatest value to me if it reaches its end." By 1899 he writes that his

Reaching Rome

Freud and his brother Alexander. Since boyhood, Freud had longed to visit Rome but some kind of internal conflict seemed to prevent him from going. Despite travelling extensively in northern and central Italy, he always made excuses for not actually getting to Rome. Ancient Rome appealed to him, but he found Christian Rome, the source of persecution suffered by his ancestors, repelled him. Freud identified with Hannibal, who was thwarted in his attempt to take Rome by some inhibition, and like Freud, never got further than Trasimeno. After four years of self-analysis, Freud finally managed to visit Rome with his brother Alexander (right). He described his visit as the "high point of my life," and would return many times.

analysis has done him a lot of good, and he is a lot more normal than he was several years previously. In 1900, he writes that he realizes that he has had a profound inner crisis, and that he has had to work through the causes of his depression.

His self-analysis was not only closely connected with his work on dreams, but also his theories of infant sexuality (see Chapter 10). Before he began his self-analysis, he was still convinced that his patients were relating stories of actual abuse in childhood. In February 1897, he remarked to Fliess that because several of his siblings showed hysterical symptoms, he thought that even his father had sexually abused his children. At this point, however, he was becoming suspicious about the frequency of such abuse, as reported to him by his patients. This suspicion was further aroused when he had a dream about his American niece, which he had to interpret as indicating a hidden sexual desire for his eldest daughter. His first two months of self-analysis, however, helped him to realize that instead of abuse, his patients were revealing their incest wishes toward their parents. While his theory of infant sexuality was not yet complete, he was at least satisfied that his father was entirely innocent of the crimes he had put against him.

Freud's self-analysis also led to his discovery of the Oedipus complex. He wrote to Fliess: "I have found, in my own case too, being in love with my mother and jealous of my father, and I now consider it a universal event in early childhood." Through his self-analysis, Freud uncovered several forgotten memories, including some significant ones, from his childhood (see Chapter 2). Some of these he confirmed with his mother, such as the memories of his old nurse that surfaced in his dreams. The nurse had been sacked after theft when he was a small child. He also examined his feelings toward his younger brother, and realized that the jealousy and ill will he had felt towards the new arrival, and rival, had led to lasting self-reproach when his wishes were fulfilled and the baby died. He also looked at his close relationship with his nephew John in his early years, and saw how this had

OPPOSITE *Amalia Freud in 1903. Freud's biographer noted that she was of a lively personality into old age, enjoying card parties "at an hour when most old ladies would be in bed."*

LEFT *Lou Andreas-Salomé (1861–1937). She trained with Freud, becoming the first female psychoanalyst. Freud became close to this intellectual woman who could count Nietzsche, Rodin, Wagner, and Tolstoy among her friends. She and Freud corresponded until her death.*

ABOVE *Freud saw Michelangelo's Moses on his first visit to Rome in 1901. Staring at it, he felt he gained an insight into Michelangelo's personality. Twelve years later he undertook a detailed study and wrote a paper that was published anonymously in* Imago.

affected the development of his character, and had determined what would be neurotic and intense in his adult friendships.

The years 1897 to 1900 saw Freud's most original and important work, and it was through his self-analysis that he formulated some of these ideas. Freud later noted that throughout his life he had to be miserable to work well, and indeed illness or malaise always seem to precede the production of his most notable work. About a passage in *The Interpretation of Dreams* he wrote, "My style in it was bad, because I was feeling too well physically; I have to be somewhat miserable in order to write well."

Freud's self-analysis formed an integral part in the formulation of psychoanalytic theory, but also aided his therapeutic work. After he began his self-analysis, he noted in 1897 that he knew his neurosis was holding him back in his therapeutic work. Overcoming his own resistances allowed him better insight into those of his patients. Once he had experienced for himself the changes of mood that they went through during treatment, he could further understand their situations. Freud would continue to analyze himself for the rest of his life, often devoting the last half hour of each day to self-analysis.

Rat Man

Ernst Lanzer entered treatment in October 1907. He had suffered obsessional thoughts, compulsive behaviors and prohibitions since childhood, which had intensified in recent years. In particular he suffered an obsessional fear that his fiancée and his father (who was actually dead) were undergoing a torture where rats are provoked to eat their way into the anus of a victim. Freud thought the obsessive ideas were produced by conflicts between Lanzer's loving and aggressive impulses to others, and were also a way of avoiding making difficult decisions in life. Lanzer's case was one of Freud's favorites, as shown by the fact he chose to keep the notes he had made throughout Lanzer's treatment when he usually destroyed them. Comparisons between the notes and published case history indicate that Freud did twist some aspects to support his theories. He considered the case a success, but sadly, Lanzer was killed in the First World War.

Freud did not take notes during sessions with patients, instead recording notable details of all the day's sessions each evening. Most of these process notes were destroyed by him, but he kept those for the complex case of Ernst Lanzer, "Rat Man." The case was one of Freud's favorites and he lectured on it while still treating Lanzer, and then presented the whole case in a four-hour talk at the first congress organized by Jung in 1908.

Interrupted by War

The early years of the new century were relatively peaceful and happy ones for Freud. His practice was thriving, though most of his patients came from outside Vienna. The years 1904 to 06 were particularly productive, and Freud published four books, *The Psychopathology of Everyday Life*, *Jokes and Their Relation to the Unconscious*, *Three Essays on Sexuality*, and the Dora case history. This was one of the peaks of creativity that Freud was convinced came about every seven years, an idea that probably came from Wilhelm Fliess's theories of cycles within life (see Chapter 7).

Despite the financial and professional stability he was now beginning to enjoy, Freud still felt he was isolated, as he had done ever since the break with Joseph Breuer (see Chapter 7) nearly a decade before – he felt shunned in Vienna and ignored abroad. This isolation would now slowly come to an end. His work began to be reviewed, particularly in England, and then in America, though Freud did not know much of this until around 1906. His ideas then began to be adopted and tested nearer to home. In 1904, Freud heard from Eugen Bleuler (1857–1939), professor of Psychiatry in Zurich, that he and his staff had been implementing psychoanalysis. The leader in this was Bleuler's assistant, Carl G. Jung (1875–1961). Jung had read *The Interpretation of Dreams* quickly after publication, and was soon applying Freud's ideas widely. In 1906, he published *The Psychology of Dementia Praecox*, which extended many of Freud's ideas into the psychoses. Freud was delighted that his researches were finding acceptance at a famous psychiatric clinic.

Support for Freud's theories also began to grow in Vienna. In the autumn of 1902, Freud invited some of those who attended his lectures at Vienna

Carl Jung (1875–1961)

After a medical degree in Basel and Zurich, Carl Gustav Jung chose to pursue a career in psychiatry. He took a position at Burghölzli Asylum under Eugen Bleuler. While there he became familiar with Freud's work, and the two shared an intense friendship until Jung's psychological theories began to diverge from Freud's. Jung would go on to form a school of psychotherapy called analytical psychology, or Jungian psychology. One of Jung's theories was that people can be classified according to psychological type, of which there are eight basic varieties – a concept which has been influential in many spheres.

" The first request of civilization ... is that of justice. "

– SIGMUND FREUD

University to meet with him to discuss his work, probably at the suggestion of one of these early followers, Wilhelm Stekel (1868–1940). The other invitees were Max Kahane (1866–1923), Rudolf Reitler (1865–1917), and Alfred Adler (1870–1937). This was the first psychoanalytic society, and it met every Wednesday in Freud's waiting room. The society was named Psychological Wednesday Society. Others joined over the following years: Otto Rank (1884–1939) in 1906, and Sándor Ferenczi (1873–1933) in 1908. Guests included Max Eitingon (1881–1943), Carl Jung and Karl Abraham (1877–1925) in 1907, Ernest Jones and A. A. Brill (1874–1948) in 1908. In 1908, the society began to collate a library, and was renamed Vienna Psychoanalytical Society.

In February 1907, Jung visited Freud. The two had been corresponding since the previous year, and would continue this for the next six years. Freud soon became very fond of Jung and decided that he would be his successor, occasionally calling him "son and heir." Jung was admiring of Freud, if not always of Freud's circle of followers.

Max Eitingon was a medical student in Zurich, and he visited Freud in 1907 to consult him on a difficult case. He visited the society, and also spent several evenings with Freud walking round the city, engrossed in personal analytic work. This was the first "training analysis" to take place. Eitingon would be very loyal to Freud for the rest of his life. Karl Abraham had worked under Bleuler and

Jung, but in 1907 he moved to Berlin to practice as a psychoanalyst. He had studied Freud's work since 1904, and had written a series of papers on psychoanalysis. Freud invited him to visit in late 1907, and so began a lasting friendship.

In 1908 Sándor Ferenczi of Budapest visited Freud. He had initially dismissed Freud's work, but on a second reading became convinced. The pair got on so well that Ferenczi was invited to spend two weeks with the Freud family that summer, the first of many holidays together. Over the next 25 years, they would exchange over 1,000 letters and from their correspondence issued several important conclusions in psychoanalysis.

In 1908, Jung organized a one-day congress in Salzburg for those interested in Freud's work. Nine papers were presented, with Freud sharing his Rat Man case history. At the congress, Ernest Jones met Freud for the first time. A Welsh neurologist, he became the first English-language practitioner of psychoanalysis and would later be Freud's biographer. He had been experimenting with hypnotic techniques in his clinical work, and in 1905 he came across Freud through reading the Dora case history.

At the congress it was decided to have further, regular congresses, and also to issue a periodical devoted to psychoanalysis. The journal – *Jahrbuch für psychoanalytische und psychopathologische Forschungen* (*Yearbook for Psycho-Analytic and Psychopathological Researches*) – would be brought out under Freud and Bleuler, and edited by Jung.

In 1909, Freud and Jung were invited to be visiting lecturers at Clark University, Worcester, Massachusetts as part of the celebrations for the university's 20th year. Freud's lectures were eagerly anticipated and he decided to give a general account of psychoanalysis. William James (1842–1910) attended his lectures, and Granville Stanley Hall (1844–1924), who was the founder of experimental psychology in America, was complimentary to both Freud and Jung. The reception was mixed, but Freud was delighted when the university conferred a doctorate on him, feeling it was a sign of recognition of his movement's work. He also met J. J. Putnam (1846–1918), professor of neurology at Harvard, and the two became friends.

Freud felt encouraged that there were men in America who understood his work, and who treated him as an equal. Although psychoanalysis was being discussed more widely in scientific and medical congresses in Europe, it was mainly being rejected. Criticisms centred on two main complaints: that

Freud's interpretations were artificial, conjured out of his own mind; and that his conclusions were repulsive or disgusting, and therefore untrue. Freud and his followers were generally considered to be not only obsessed with sex but psychopaths who presented a danger to society. Freud was the main target, but his followers were attacked as well. Freud didn't take this opposition particularly to heart, but did decry the arrogance, rudeness, and illogicality of his critics. He did seem sensitive, however, to accusations that he had made up his theories.

In the face of such opposition, Freud was keen to bring analysts closer together, and he asked Sándor Ferenczi to address the second International Psychoanalytical Congress in March 1910, at Nuremberg, about how analysts and their work might be organized in the future. An international association was formed, composed of local societies under Jung as president.

Branches of the International Psycho-Analytical Association (IPA) were beginning to flourish across

Europe. The American Psychoanalytic Association was established in 1911, and news reached Freud that a group were studying his writings in Australia. Freud started *Imago* in 1911 to allow the publication of papers and articles devoted to the non-medical applications of psychoanalysis, a move which followed his broadening interests. Despite all this progress, dissension within the psychoanalysis movement would soon sorely wound Freud.

Alfred Adler had been associated with Freud since 1902, and was now president of the Vienna Society, but he was developing very different ideas to Freud's. Freud considered Adler was "developing backwards," as he rejected several of Freud's key concepts. Adler had always felt it important to treat a patient as a whole person, and in relation to their environment. As his holistic approach developed, Freud's increasing insistence on dividing up a person into concepts did not sit well with Adler, and his contention that the "social realm" was as important to psychology as the "internal realm" did not fit into Freud's ideas. Adler increasingly downplayed the Freudian concept that neuroses stem from sexual conflicts in childhood. Freud also did not share Adler's socialist beliefs.

Their separation was quite protracted, and Freud did consider and discuss Adler's ideas. In early 1911, following heated debates, Adler and Stekel resigned as president and vice-president. A few months later, Adler left the society altogether. Freud suggested that he step down as editor of the journal *Zentralblatt für Psychoanalyse*. Adler insisted on an extraordinary meeting. He had formed a group called Society for Free Psychoanalysis, claiming he was fighting for the freedom of science. At the meeting, members had to decide which society they wished to belong to. The split finally made official, Adler's adherents went with him to the new society. Wilhelm Stekel also resigned from the society in 1911. Freud's biographer wrote that Freud was relieved after Adler and Stekel had left the society, as it was an end to a difficult and unpleasant time.

After splitting with Freud, Adler established the Society of Individual Psychology in 1912. Also in 1912, Adler published *Über den Nervösen Charakter* (*The Neurotic Constitution*), in which he discussed his ideas, and which developed into his school of "individual psychology." Adler later founded a number of child guidance clinics in Vienna that became a prototype for similar clinics elsewhere,

LEFT *Freud with his sons Ernst and Martin in 1916, both of whom were on active service at the time.*

as he felt that personality problems should be addressed in childhood to have the most impact, both for the child and society. His ideas have found broad acceptance within psychology, and have had a wide influence.

Jung had founded the Freud Society in Zurich in 1907, and had been a valuable defender of Freudian theories for several years. Freud had hoped Carl Jung would succeed him and act as a focus for all psychoanalytical activities, but Jung prefered to work alone on his own interests. Despite Freud's high hopes and fondness for Jung, he noted that his personal research interests interfered with his presidential duties, and soon realized that he must lessen his expectations of Jung.

As a background to the Freud–Jung affair, it should be noted that there had always been a degree of antipathy between the Viennese analysts and the Swiss contingent. Jung's admiration for Freud had never embraced his group of followers in Vienna, and the ill-feeling between Vienna and Switzerland only increased over the period until

Jung's break with Freud. Also, public outrage against Freud's sexual theories in Switzerland had put a lot of pressure on Swiss analysts to reject the wickedness invading their country from Vienna.

Jung's main disagreement with Freud was over their concepts of the unconscious. While he acknowledged Freud's model, which he called the "personal unconscious," Jung proposed a second, deeper form of the unconscious underlying the personal unconscious. This was the "collective unconscious," where Jung's archetypes resided: universal inherited models of people or behaviors. Jung also saw the libido as a kind of life force, rejecting Freud's theory that it was necessarily a sexual energy. Overall, he saw behavior affected by abstract, even spiritual processes, rather than sexual drives. Jung had always felt that it was unnecessary to "go into unsavory details" in analysis, and his rejection of Freud's sexual theories fitted the model of psychoanalysis he was developing.

As Jung worked on his *Wandlungen und Symbole der Libido* (*Psychology of the Unconscious*), the differences

Jones   Eitingon   SF   Rank

between Jung's and Freud's theories, particularly on the nature of libido and religion, became even more apparent. The publication of the book in 1912 was an irreversible step in the two men's separation. As well as their intellectual differences, Jung also recorded that he disliked Freud's determination to preserve the theories of psychoanalysis as unquestioned articles of faith.

Their personal separation widened in 1912, with Freud feeling that Jung was snubbing him, and Jung choosing to lecture at Fordham University, New York in September, causing the congress to be postponed to the following year. While in America, Jung made comments about Freud's theories, and Freud, being out of date. Later that year, the two men agreed to discontinue their personal correspondence, however Jung was still president of the IPA and editor of the *Jahrbuch*.

During the first half of 1913, Freud was working on *Totem and Taboo*, which he expected would increase the gap between himself and Jung; and he told Ferenczi that it would divide "us" – Vienna

and Zurich – "as an acid does a salt." Shortly after, he reconsidered, saying that he didn't really want a split, preferring Jung to leave of his own accord. That summer, Freud still wanted to try and avoid a formal break with Jung and the Swiss, despite Jung's renunciation of the main concepts of psychoanalysis. At the congress in Munich in September 1913, Jones read a paper that directly criticized Jung's theories, which Freud had approved before the congress. When Jung's name came up for re-election as president at the congress, Abraham suggested that those who disapproved should abstain from voting, and a total of 22 abstained.

The 1913 Munich Congress was the final break between the two men, who would never meet again. The following April, Jung resigned from editorship of *Jahrbuch*, from the presidency, and then later that year, from the society itself. Practically all the Swiss – with the notable exception of Oskar Pfister – joined Jung, and the Zurich Society withdrew from the IPA in July.

Freud knew that Jung's defection would harm psychoanalysis. Jung was received well by many because he had removed the sexual elements of psychoanalysis, precisely the theories which had proved so repugnant to most people. Other critics said that if there were three schools of psychoanalysis which could not agree, then it was not necessary for anyone else to take it at all seriously. Particularly in answer to the claim that there were many conflicting kinds of psychoanalysis, Freud wrote *History of the Psycho-Analytical Movement* in early 1914.

During all this turmoil, Ernest Jones suggested that a small group of "trusted" analysts and followers be established around Freud, to protect him in the case of further dissensions, and to further support his work. The only obligation for these followers

LEFT *International Psychoanalytical Conference, Hague, 1920. Ernest Jones, Freud, and Otto Rank, all in the second row back, are labelled. On Freud's right is Oskar Pfister. Sándor Ferenczi sits in the middle of the front row and Anna Freud sits third from left.*

was that if they wished to depart from any major parts of psychoanalytic theory, they should discuss their views with the rest before airing them publicly. Freud was enthusiastic about a "guard" for his creation, and the Committee first met in summer 1913. The original members were Otto Rank, Hanns Sachs (1881–1947), Sándor Ferenczi, and Karl Abraham, with Ernest Jones as chairman.

Between 1911 and 1915, Freud published several papers on techniques in psychoanalysis, with practical recommendations for analysts. Freud felt that the dissensions with the movement were the result mainly of an imperfect knowledge of the technique, and so he hoped to further safeguard the movement with these papers. He discusses remembering all the names and facts for each case, particularly when seeing several patients in a day. He advises against taking full notes during sessions. He also advised against working on a case scientifically while treatment was ongoing. The analyst was not to introduce his or her own thoughts or information about their own life into the psychoanalytic process, as that would verge on treatment by suggestion, and would make it harder for the patient to uncover their own unconscious thoughts. He also supplied suggestions on fees, times, duration of treatments, and other practical matters. Through these and other methods, he was trying to create an institutional framework for psychoanalysis that would endure after his death.

But war would interrupt Freud's plans for psychoanalysis. In June 1914, the assassination of Archduke Franz Ferdinand of Austria, in Sarajevo, Serbia, sparked off a chain of events that resulted in the First World War. By August, Austria-Hungary was at war, allied with the German and Ottoman Empires, against France, the British and Russian Empires, Japan, Belgium, and Serbia.

Freud was initially in favor of the war, but soon returned to his previous, pacifist, stance after witnessing Germany's incompetence against Serbia, and realizing that the war would be protracted.

After war broke out, patients were scarce, and visitors to distract him from the war were few and far between. All three of Freud's sons went on active service and several analysts were called up as doctors. He tried his best to keep the psychoanalytic journals – all that was left of the psychoanalytical movement – going, by writing papers to fill them, reducing their size and eventually producing them less frequently. The *Jahrbuch* folded in 1914. Ferenczi did manage to visit Vienna occasionally, but Freud felt increasingly alone as the war raged on. However, in this renewed isolation, and suffering low spirits, Freud's productivity soared, even though, as he wrote to Ferenczi, "I know that I am writing for only

Freud's visit to the USA

In September 1909, Freud made his only visit to the United States. After this visit, psychoanalysis became very popular in America among the public, and recognized by psychiatrists, but Freud said in 1920 it had been "watered down." Despite the honor paid him at Clark University, Freud did not form a good opinion of the United States. He complained that American cooking had a lasting effect on his digestion, and for several years blamed many of his physical ailments on the trip. Front, from left: Freud, Granville Stanley Hall, Carl Jung; back from left: Abraham A. Brill, Ernest Jones, Sándor Ferenczi.

five people in the present, you and the few others [Abraham, Rank, Sachs and Jones]."

The stretches of free time Freud now had led him to work on a major book on metapsychology. He had long thought of writing a summary of his psychoanalytic theories, and in March 1915 he began his series of papers with "Instincts and their Vicissitudes," "Repression," "The Unconscious," "The Metapsychological Supplement of the Theory of Dreams," and "Mourning and Melancholia," which were all published. By the end of that summer he had completed all 12 of the papers that were to make up the book, however the final seven did not survive. He seems to have destroyed them, perhaps after the war when he began to rethink some of his theories. The paper on the unconscious was his favourite, and by far the longest, published in two parts in the *Zeitschrift* in late 1915.

During the war, Freud gave a series of lectures at Vienna University to physicians and laymen. Published in 1916–1917 as *Vorlesungen zur Einführung in die Psychoanalyse* (*Introductory Lectures on Psychoanalysis*) they were an immense success. Within Freud's lifetime, 50,000 copies were sold in German. It has been translated into at least 15 languages.

Other papers resulted from his reflections on the war and devastation around him, such as *Zeitgemässes über Krieg und Tod* (*Thoughts for the Times on War and Death*). It comprises two essays, one on disillusionment, and the other on the altered attitude to death that war provokes.

As the war progressed, food shortages and closed frontiers meant a more dismal life for many Austrians, including Freud and his family. Freud also complained in his letters about the bitter cold and how the tension of the situation stopped him from writing. He was becoming increasingly pessimistic about the outcome of the war, and by late 1917, he had lost all sympathy for Germany, and felt that the war was lost. By 1918, he and most Austrians realized that they were in it to the "bitter end" with Germany. That summer a congress was held in Budapest, masterminded by Abraham.

BELOW *An etching of Freud produced in 1914 by Germain Jewish artist Hermann Struck, complete with Freud's signature in the corner. In November 1914, Freud wrote to Struck to say that he admired his serious approach to working on the portrait.*

Representatives of the Austrian, German, and Hungarian governments attended, because of their interest in "war neuroses." Abraham, Eitingon, and Ferenczi had been undertaking practical work with soldiers, which had been noted by high-ranking army medical officers, and there was talk of psychoanalytical clinics for those suffering war neuroses.

Finally, in November 1918, the end came, and Austro-Hungary signed an armistice with Italy. The Austria-Hungarian Empire was dissolved and broken up into several new states, with Vienna now just the capital of the republic of Austria.

Freud's *Zur Einführung des Narzissmus* (*On Narcissism*), published 1914. The paper is a turning point in Freud's thinking on the drives. He suggests there is an "ego-libido" and "object-libido," an idea which breaks down his previous division between the ego drives which are not erotic, and the libidinal drives which are not egotistic. The paper also introduces the "ego ideal." Over the following 10 years Freud would completely restructure his theory of the mind.

Death of a Daughter

Life in Vienna after the end of the First World War was a world away from the life and culture of the city of Freud's youth. Thin vegetable soup was the staple diet, owing to continued food shortages, and there was very limited heating or lighting. All three of Freud's sons survived the war and returned home, although the family had to wait months for news of Martin, who was a prisoner of war in Italy. Freud's nephew (his sister Rosa's son), Hermann Graf, killed in Italy aged 20, was the only loss in the family.

In the final years of the war, Freud had begun to fear that with his falling income, he might end up bankrupt. After the war ended, his practice improved, and he treated far more patients. Economic prospects in Austria were bleak, however, and Freud had to help his sons and the rest of his family, even though his earnings were now being outpaced by inflation. He had to spend all his savings in the first years after the war, leaving him with nothing for his old age.

He realized that he needed foreign – specifically English and American – patients who could pay him in their own currency. Ernest Jones (see Chapter 12) sent him patients, upon whose fees Freud became quite reliant. Would-be analysts were soon flocking from the west to learn his technique, but analyzing and teaching in a foreign language was hard work, and by the end of a working day Freud was exhausted. Despite all these efforts, his finances didn't start to recover until a couple of years after the war.

The war had stimulated interest in psychoanalysis in Germany and the West because of "war neuroses." In early 1920, Freud was asked to submit evidence to a commission on the treatment of war neurotics by Austrian military doctors, especially at Vienna General Hospital. He examined the use of electrical

Marie Bonaparte (1882–1962)

Marie Bonaparte was a descendant of Napoleon's brother and heiress to a great fortune. In 1907 she married Prince George of Greece and Denmark, and had two children with him. In the 1920s, she researched female sexuality, publishing the results anonymously. In 1925 she consulted Freud regarding her own condition. She later trained as an analyst, becoming a leading figure in the international psychoanalytical movement, and translating Freud's work into French. She became lifelong friends with Freud and his family, and helped both the psychoanalytical movement, and the Freud family financially.

RIGHT *Freud and Ernest Jones (left) after the war, in Austria. Jones and Freud remained in contact during the war, with their correspondence travelling via neutral countries, but were unable to meet until late 1919, when Jones managed to visit Vienna, one of the first foreigners to do so.*

treatment, which had been introduced by the German army, and was initially deemed successful because patients were prepared to go back to the front to avoid further treatment. However, they would soon "relapse" when they got there. As the war progressed, stronger currents and more severe treatments were used, which resulted in some deaths and suicides. Freud concluded that he was quite

sure the head of the Vienna Psychiatric Division would not have allowed such cruel treatment, but couldn't vouch for other doctors, or judge whether treatment had become more severe during the war. His inclusion in the inquiry reflected the regard for his position in Vienna at the time, but when he was asked to give evidence in front of the commission, it didn't end well. Freud's opinions – that while

ABOVE *Sophie Freud and Max Halberstadt in 1913, at around the time of their marriage.*

psychoanalysis was difficult to apply during wartime, it would have been more successful than electric treatment, and that doctors would have been conflicted between the best interests of the patient and the requirement to get the patient back fighting as soon as possible – led to the hearing becoming a debate. The commission ranged against Freud, and harsh criticism of psychoanalysis only confirmed Freud's opinion of Viennese psychiatrists.

Despite the situation in Vienna, the continued lack of favor toward his work in Austria and Germany, and the separation from the Hungarian centre of psychoanalysis because of political events, Freud was cheered by the fact that the international psychoanalytic movement was re-establishing itself in the post-war era.

Plans for centers to treat war neuroses came to nothing in the midst of the political chaos after the war, but following discussions at the Budapest Congress in 1918, and owing to the generosity of Max Eitingon (see Chapter 12), the first

psychoanalytical polyclinic was opened in Berlin in 1920, with buildings designed by Ernst.

The center brought together therapy, research, and training under one roof. Freud felt that this made Berlin the chief psychoanalytical center. A similar clinic opened in Vienna in 1922, rather against Freud's wishes, since he felt that Vienna was not a suitable center for psychoanalysis, and so unsuitable for such a clinic.

There was much talk of Freud's work in England, where Jones reorganized the London Psycho-Analytical Society into the British Psycho-Analytical Society in 1919. Jones and Sándor Ferenczi had managed, not without difficulty, to get to Vienna to see Freud in 1919, at which time Freud had decided that the center of the movement needed to move west, and the acting presidency of the IPA was transferred from Ferenczi to Jones. Freud's Introductory Lectures appeared in English in America in 1919 – arranged by his nephew Edward Bernays (1891–1995) – and a separate English translation, produced by Joan Riviere (1883–1962), appeared in England in 1922.

Among those who flocked to Vienna after the war were James (1887–1967) and Alix (1892–1973) Strachey. The couple were part of the Bloomsbury Group, the members of which had been interested in Freud and psychoanalysis since before the First World War. James became a student of Freud in 1920, undertaking two years of analysis before returning to London and becoming an analyst himself. Alix was later analyzed by Karl Abraham (see Chapter 12) in Berlin and also became an analyst. While they were in Vienna, Freud, who was already familiar with the work of James' older brother Lytton Strachey (1880–1932), asked the Stracheys to translate some of his works into English and help spread psychoanalysis in Britain. James became an influential teacher and analyst,

ABOVE *A photograph of Freud and Sophie in 1913, taken in Hamburg by Sophie's husband Max.*

but he and Alix became increasingly engrossed in translating Freud's works, in collaboration with Ernest Jones and Joan Riviere. They translated the third volume of Freud's *Collected Papers*, and after Freud's death James, with Alix's assistance, would prepare the standard edition of Freud's writings in English, in 24 volumes.

The first post-war congress was held in Holland in September 1920. Holland was chosen because it was a neutral country, and Freud, who attended with his daughter Anna, was moved by how hospitable the Dutch were to the "starving and impoverished subjects of the Central European states." The congress was deemed a success, with many of the 62 members present (from America, England, Germany, Holland, Hungary, Austria, Poland, and Switzerland) meeting for the first time after many years divided by war.

Also, in early 1919, Vienna saw the opening of a publishing house dedicated to the publication of psychoanalytical works – the Internationaler Psychoanalytischer Verlag – mainly the result of the generosity of Freud's good friend Anton (Toni) von Freund (1880–1920), although von Freund's grant would lose much of its value because of post-war inflation. The first directors were Freud, von Freund, Ferenczi, and Rank. The establishment of the Verlag meant that Freud no longer had to worry about the vagaries of publishing houses, and could publish what and when he wanted. It also helped secure the continuance of the psychoanalytical periodicals. Over the 20 years of its existence it would publish more than 150 books, all on psychoanalysis. It was rarely solvent, however. Freud never took royalties for his books, and in fact he put much of his own money into the Verlag. Other authors had to help subsidize the cost of producing their books as well. Into the 1920s, translation of Freud's works into many languages were being arranged by the Verlag.

These signs of rejuvenation and growth after the war would soon be overshadowed by the sad events of 1920. On January 20, 1920, Toni von Freund died after a long illness. Freud had visited him every day during the last months of his illness, and comforted him as best he could. Freud was very fond of him, and his death was a blow. But tragedy would soon strike Freud much closer to home.

Two of Freud's daughters were now married – Mathilde, who had married Robert Hollitscher in 1909, and Sophie. Sophie was Freud's "Sunday child," his fifth child. She was her mother's favorite, and much loved and admired by Freud. In 1912, aged 19, Sophie had announced her engagement to Max Halberstadt (1882–1940), a well-known Jewish photographer in Hamburg. Though perhaps hoping to keep her at home a little longer, her

Like father, like daughter

Interested in psychoanalysis as a young teenager, Anna Freud was allowed to listen to the discussions and papers each Wednesday evening. In 1918, Freud began to train her as a psychoanalyst, undertaking her analysis himself, which at that time was unusual, but not yet unacceptable. She read a formal paper to the Vienna Society in 1922 to become an accredited member. Anna would also learn a great deal from Lou Andreas-Salomé (1861–1937), and a quasi-analytical relationship would develop between them. Here, Freud and Anna are shown at the 1920 Congress.

parents were not unhappy at the news. Freud wrote to Halberstadt: "My little Sophie ... broke the surprising news that she is engaged to you. We realize that this fact makes us, so to speak, superfluous and that there is nothing left for us to do but go through the formality of bestowing our blessing." Halberstadt was 30, a distant relative to the Freud family, and Martha and Minna knew him and his family. The couple married in early 1913, and settled in Hamburg. The following year they welcomed their first child, Ernst Wolfgang. Another son, Heinz, known as Heinele, was born in 1918.

Freud visited Sophie in September 1919, on his way home from taking "the cure" at Bad Gastein; it would be the last time he saw her. Just four months later, news reached Freud and Martha, on the evening of von Freund's burial, that Sophie was seriously ill, a victim of the great influenza pandemic that was ravaging Europe and the United States. Freud and Martha were unable to get to her as there were no trains running from Vienna to Germany, and just a few days later, this active young mother was dead at the age of just 26.

Freud wrote to his friend Pastor Oskar Pfister, "The loss of a child seems to be a serious, narcissistic injury; what is known as mourning will probably follow only later." He wrote to Sándor Ferenczi that for years he had prepared himself for the loss of his sons, but now it was his daughter who had been taken. He commented to several people that he had no one to accuse, for he was not religious, and as such was spared the conflicts that a believer would suffer on the death of a loved one.

Freud's name and work were now becoming more widely known than ever, and at times he felt his increasing popularity to be burdensome, as it added considerably to his correspondence. Professionally, he was very busy, taking on fewer patients because he also had so many pupils to teach. Interest in psychoanalysis in Vienna was finally reaching wider circles, and he was invited to many lectures. With so many demands on his time and energy, he felt that old age was beginning to catch him up as he turned 65 in 1921. There were moments of family happiness

as he and Martha welcomed three new grandsons in the early 1920s, and he was proud when his daughter Anna Freud was made a member of the Vienna Society in June 1922 (see Chapter 20). But that summer his 23-year-old niece Caecilie, of whom he was very fond, overdosed on Veronal after finding herself pregnant. She was the only daughter of Freud's favorite sister Rosa, whose only son, Hermann, had been killed during the war. Freud was shaken by the tragedy.

In September 1922, Freud went to the Berlin Congress. It would be the last one that he would attend. In February 1923, he noticed a growth on the right side of his jaw and palate. He consulted physician friends, Maxim Steiner and Felix Deutsch (1884–1964), who was also his personal doctor. It is said that Deutsch realized that it was cancer, but told Freud it was a leucoplakia. Both urged him to see a surgeon. Finally in April he consulted a rhinologist, Marcus Hajek (1861–1941), who diagnosed it as a leucoplakia, caused by smoking. Hajek recommended it be removed, and so a few days later Freud turned up at the outpatient clinic, without mentioning it to anyone at home. Unfortunately, the operation did not go as planned, and Martha was surprised to get a phone message asking her to take in the necessities for Freud to have an overnight stay. He suffered further bleeding, but next day was allowed home.

The growth was found to be cancerous, but Freud was not told of this. Hajek, a mediocre surgeon perhaps, had not taken precautions against the scar shrinking, so the opening of Freud's mouth was reduced and caused him continued difficulties. Freud then underwent treatments involving x-rays, and then a series of treatments with radium capsules. These were drastic measures, and he suffered from side effects.

Around the time of Freud's operation, his grandson, Heinz Halberstadt, Sophie's son, had his tonsils removed. Heinz had been spending some time in Vienna with his aunt Mathilde, and Freud was very fond of him, calling him the most intelligent child he had ever encountered. Heinz was

a delicate boy; his grandfather once wrote, "He was very weak, never entirely free of a temperature, one of those children whose mental development grows at the expense of its physical strength." In 1922 he contracted tuberculosis and the following year he fell ill again. After several weeks without a diagnosis, the family were told that he had miliary tuberculosis, and nothing could be done. On June 19, he died, aged just four and a half. The loss hit Freud harder than previous family deaths, and it was the only time in his life that he was known to have cried. His letters show that he found the blow unbearable, much worse than the death of his daughter, or his own cancer, and he later said he formed no new attachments after Heinz's death, no longer enjoying life and becoming indifferent to his own fate.

Though Hajek allowed Freud to go on his customary three-month holiday that summer, he required his patient to send a report of his condition every two weeks and instructed him to visit him halfway through the holiday, which alarmed Freud. Hajek then said Freud need not visit him, which increased Freud's distrust of his surgeon. During his time away, Freud's discomfort was such that he asked Felix Deutsch to visit him. Deutsch realized the growth had returned, and Freud would need a further, more radical operation. He didn't tell him this as he feared Freud, deep in mourning for Heinz, might refuse, preferring to die, and he was also reluctant to doom a much-anticipated trip to Rome with Anna. The committee were informed, and discussed if and how to tell Freud. Freud was furious to find out later that they had considered not telling him. Hajek, even after seeing the pathology report, assured Freud that the growth was not malignant, but arrangements were made for an operation on his return to Vienna from Rome. While he was away with Anna, Deutsch persuaded a distinguished oral surgeon, Hans Pichler, to take charge of the case. When Freud returned from Rome, he was finally told the truth.

On September 26, Pichler and Hajek examined Freud's mouth, and found a malignant ulcer in the hard palate that had invaded the upper part of the lower jaw, and the cheek. Radical action was needed. The major operation was carried out in two stages, on October 4 and 11, 1923. Under local anaesthetic, Pichler removed the whole upper jaw and palate on the right side, which meant that the mouth and nasal cavity were now one. Freud made a good recovery and returned home at the end of the month. Traces of cancerous material were found, necessitating a further operation in November, which caused severe bleeding. Further x-ray treatments had to be endured over the next few weeks.

The following 16 years would be filled with pain and discomfort, with over 30 operations to try and combat Freud's cancer of the mouth. To replace his palate, a large prosthesis was made, dubbed "the monster" by Freud. It had to fit tightly so was difficult to wear, and was constantly irritating and sore, despite regular adjustments. It also prevented tissues and ulcers from healing. If it was left out for even a few hours, the tissues could shrink, which meant that it could not be replaced without alteration. Further prosthetics were made the next year, but without much success.

Freud's speech was greatly affected by the operations and prostheses, becoming nasal and thick. It was difficult to eat, and he seldom did so in company. His hearing was also affected by the operations, and he became almost deaf in his right ear. Over time, the adrenaline used in relation to his operations began to affect his heart. He was allowed to continue smoking, but he had to force his jaw open with a clothes peg in order to get a cigar between his teeth.

Karl Abraham (1877–1925)

Karl Abraham first met Freud in 1907. He was an original member of the committee, and was president of the IPA from 1914–1918 and in 1925. He analyzed Melanie Klein (1882–1960) and several other British psychoanalysts, including Alix Strachey. He was a mentor to an influential group of German analysts, including Karen Horney (1885–1952). In particular, Abraham investigated stages of childhood psychosexual development, and linked different mental illnesses to the point at which this development is fixated. Unlike many of those close to Freud, Abraham remained a friend until his premature death. He died on Christmas Day 1925 from an undiagnosed illness, most likely lung cancer.

BELOW *Amalie Freud on her 90th birthday in 1925 with her daughters. Standing behind are Pauli (Winternitz), Dolfi (Freud), and Mitzi (Moritz-Freud). On her left is Rosa (Graf), and to her right Anna (Bernays).*

Freud refused to have anyone nurse him at any point in his illness except his daughter Anna. They made a pact at the very beginning that she would perform all that was necessary with no emotion. She would continue to do so right until his death. Freud found it difficult to forgive the way that the truth had been kept from him that summer. Deutsch realized this, and even though he had acted from the best of intentions, some months after the operations, he told Freud that he could no longer be his doctor.

Freud finally returned to work in early 1924. He resumed seeing six patients, but found it very difficult as talking was so tiring. He admitted that he was tempted to give up all work and wait "for the natural end," but felt it necessary to continue to earn since he continued to spend. (This was partly because he insisted on paying all his doctors, rather than accepting the professional courtesy then usual between physicians.) He published five papers in the year. The following year he had further operations, and couldn't travel far from Vienna because he needed to stay close to his surgeon. However, at this time almost anyone who visited Vienna would aim to visit Freud, and so he was kept occupied. In September of that year, Anna would read a paper by Freud at the Homburg Congress.

The year 1924 saw dissension within the committee, centering on Otto Rank. His publication of *The Development of Psychoanalysis* with Sándor Ferenczi in 1923 had caused some ripples, as Freud did not fully agree with what it contained even though he had read it before publication. Rank's book *The Trauma of Birth* late that year caused more issues. Freud had not seen it before publication. Rank's main theme was that life consisted of endeavors to surmount or undo the trauma of birth, and it was the failure of these attempts that caused neurosis. Analysis could therefore be focused on the theme of trauma at birth, and completed in a few months. Freud's opinion on Rank's ideas changed more than once, and the opinions of other members of the Committee were varied, but mainly negative. The result was that the Committee was temporarily disbanded in spring 1924. Freud made the mistake of telling Rank that Karl Abraham felt the two books showed a regression similar to that of Carl Jung. Both Rank and Ferenczi were furious. In 1924, Rank went to America, and reports soon reached Europe that he was teaching his own new theories of psychoanalysis. When Rank returned to Vienna, Freud saw him, but their talk was inconclusive. Rank then left for America again, but on his way, he was seized with depression in Paris, and returned to Vienna. He was again a changed man, and attributed his previous behavior to a neurosis. Freud was overjoyed that his friend had been returned to him. Rank wrote to the members of the committee explaining and apologizing. In late 1924, the committee reformed, with Anna Freud taking the place of Rank. Rank stopped short of renouncing his new theories, and spent much of his remaining life in America, emigrating there in 1935.

From the mid-1920s, the features of the psychoanalytical movement that most interested Freud were the Verlag, and the question of lay analysts. While all analysts had initially been qualified doctors, Freud did not feel that a medical qualification was necessary, and welcomed non-doctors for training. For him the core of training to become a psychoanalyst was to undergo analysis oneself, and several of his patients, such as Marie Bonaparte, went on to become psychoanalysts in their own right. He thought that lay analysts should not operate independently, but only work with patients first seen, and referred to them, by a doctor. In some countries, such as the United States, however, it was illegal for any therapeutic work to be carried out by those without a medical qualification, and the question of whether or not lay analysts should be allowed became a heated issue within the International Psycho-Analytical Association (IPA). Freud wrote a paper on the debate in 1926, advocating a liberal attitude to lay analysis, but the debate rumbled on, with the New York Society condemning lay analysis in 1927, and the Innsbruck Congress that year seeing a heated debate between Vienna and New York. The problem would still be unresolved at the time of Freud's death.

In 1926, Freud suffered further health problems, but this time with his heart. He was diagnosed with myocarditis caused by an intolerance to tobacco, which made him give up smoking temporarily. He was forced to spend a month in a cottage sanatorium, from where he treated three patients, and he then lived a semi-invalid life back in Vienna. His accumulating illnesses made him consider again how much longer he could work – particularly as he was no longer smoking, and he had always considered smoking crucial to his writing – and also how long he might live. On his 70th birthday around 10 of his pupils presented him with a birthday gift of 30,000 marks from the members of the association. He made a speech to them in which he said that they must regard him as retired from active participation in the psychoanalytical movement. The following day he held his last meeting with the committee. Despite his pessimism, or realism, Freud would live, and work, for many more years.

The Ego, Super-Ego, and Id

In spite of his physical illnesses, and self-professed fatigue with life, Freud continued to produce new and exciting thoughts in the 1920s, revisiting and quite drastically revising some of his older theories. One key strand in his thinking at this time was a systematic study of the ego. His new phase of work on the ego began with *Massenpsychologie und Ich-analyse* (*Group Psychology and the Analysis of the Ego*), in 1921.

At the Berlin Congress in 1922, Freud presented some new ideas in a paper called "Some Remarks on the Unconscious." These were taken from his book *The Ego and the Id*, which he published in 1923, and which he described as further developing some trains of thought from *Beyond the Pleasure Principle* (see Chapter 15). In this book, Freud presented his heavily revised model of structures and functions of the mind, incorporating the id, the ego, and the super-ego. While he didn't abandon his earlier topography of the conscious, preconscious, and unconscious (see Chapter 9), he saw it as less critical than before. Previously he felt that the ego stood in opposition to the unconscious, but he now felt that much of the ego was unconscious. The book is without doubt the decisive work for Freud's later years.

The "id," which comes from the Latin word for "it," was, for Freud, the primary source of psychic energy, the primary component of personality, and fully unconscious. It is driven by the pleasure principle, striving to obtain what it wants and

ABOVE *Arthur Schopenhauer (1788–1860), German philosopher. Schopenhauer's concept of the "will" is strikingly similar to Freud's idea of the unconscious and id. However, Freud maintained he only read Schopenhauer's books late in life, and the similarities between their work are mere coincidence.*

OPPOSITE *The cover of* Das Ich und das Es *(The Ego and the Id), 1923, published by the newly established Verlag.*

Das Ich und das Es

von

Sigm. Freud

1.—8. Tausend

Internationaler
Psychoanalytischer Verlag

Leipzig   Wien   Zürich

LEFT Freud (center) at Tegel Sanatorium in Berlin in the late 1920s for treatment. He was suffering intense pain in his mouth by 1928, and was encouraged by his son Ernst to consult a famous surgeon in Berlin, Professor Schroeder. He went to the Tegel Sanatorium for the first time in late August 1928, accompanied by Anna. In November, he returned to Vienna with a new, improved prosthesis. He would be treated at Tegel several more times.

needs, right now. The id is the only one of the three components which is present at birth, thus a baby's behavior is ruled by the id. A baby who is hungry or unhappy will cry until his or her needs are met. There is no negotiation or recognition of the limitations of what is possible, it is simply the id demanding what it wants and needs.

As children develop and interact with the external world, they become more aware of being separate and different from other humans. This is when the ego develops. Before Freud, the word "ego," Latin for "I," had usually meant "the self," the subject of consciousness, and object of the individual's self-consciousness. Freud had started considering the "self" in the early days of psychoanalysis, but in his new, open structure of the mind he labelled the agency of the mind that was open to the external world as "the I" (das Ich), which his English translator James Strachey turned into the Latinized "ego," Freud's original terms, das Es, das Ich, and das Über-Ich – the It, the I, and the Over-I – were far more self-explanatory to the German reader than the English terms. The ego operates on the "reality principle": it understands the limitations

of what is possible in the external world, and how to go about getting round these limitations. The ego is present in the conscious, preconscious, and unconscious. Freud considered the ego to develop from the id, and the two were intimately related, with the lower portion of the ego merging into the id. The repressed also merges into the id, and can only communicate with the ego through the id, with resistances of repression keeping it in check. Freud wrote, "We shall look upon the individual as a psychical id, unknown and unconscious, upon whose surface rests the ego."

As a child grows, his or her ego develops from that part of the id which has been shaped by the external world. The ego aims to try and fulfil the urges of the id, but in realistic ways that are appropriate to the external environment. The costs and benefits of action are considered before an urge is indulged, which is quite different to the id's wish to immediately grab what it wants, regardless of the consequences. If necessary, the ego will delay gratification, allowing the fulfilment of the id's urges only at a time and place that is appropriate. As Freud put it, "The ego represents what may be

106 SIGMUND FREUD: THE MAN, THE SCIENTIST, AND THE BIRTH OF PSYCHOANALYSIS

> **"** *The ego is not master in its own house.* **"**

> – SIGMUND FREUD

called reason and common sense, in contrast to the id, which contains the passions." If the urges of the id cannot be met, the ego also tries to discharge the tension this creates.

The final element of the personality to develop is the super-ego, which develops out of the ego at around the age of five. The super-ego is an internal sense of right and wrong, which aims to perfect a person's behavior. Initially, parents or an authority figure provide children with standards, or a "higher nature" that, as a child grows, they internalize. The super-ego works to make the ego act in accordance with ideal standards, rather than the reality principle. As with the ego, the super-ego is present in the conscious, preconscious, and unconscious. Freud would later describe the super-ego's functions as "self-observation, of conscience and of the ideal." Freud thought that the super-ego "contains the germ from which all religions have evolved."

Freud considered the development of the super-ego to be part of the outcome of the sexual phase dominated by the Oedipus complex (see Chapter 10)

Freud's cigars

Smoking was certainly an addiction for Freud, who averaged 20 cigars a day, once proclaiming "smoking is one of the greatest and cheapest enjoyments in life." He smoked as he analyzed, walked, and wrote, and he made daily visits to his tobacconist. Even after the diagnosis of his mouth cancer he continued to smoke cigars, apart from some temporary breaks, usually because of his cardiac complications. He knew they were killing him, but he was convinced that they enabled him to work much better. After his 75th birthday he decided he ought not to be refused anything, by which time he couldn't find suitable cigars in Austria, so friends went to great lengths to meet his needs.

LEFT *Freud and Anna at Tegel in 1929. As Freud's health declined, not only did Anna begin to represent him internationally, but she became his main nurse and aide. She was devoted to her father, and he was overwhelmingly appreciative of her care.*

– in fact to be part of the repression of the Oedipus complex. The child's parents, particularly the father, are seen as the obstacle to the realization of Oedipal wishes, so the child's ego strengthens itself to perform the necessary repression by recreating the same obstacles within itself. He felt that the female super-ego was never as strong as that of the male.

Freud described the ego as being like a rider sitting on a horse, the horse being the id. The rider uses the energy of the horse, but also has to defend itself against the forces of the horse, which could throw it off. Later attempts to fit the super-ego into this story have resulted in the analogy of a horse and chariot. The id is the horse, unevolved and instinctual. The ego is the rational driver of the chariot, able to guide the id, but never managing to gain complete control, since the horse can overpower him. The super-ego is the father of the chariot driver, sitting beside him, pointing out where he is going wrong.

Freud considered that the id could be inherited, and that experiences of the ego, if repeated often enough and strongly enough by individuals in successive generations, could be transformed into experiences of the id, and therefore the id could harbor "residues of the resistances of countless egos." He was fascinated by how these three aspects of the mind interact and come into conflict, with the ego trying to satisfy the id, within the limitations imposed by the super-ego, while also dealing with the external world. He described the ego as "a poor creature owing service to three masters and consequently menaced by three dangers: from the external world, from the libido of the id and from the severity of the super-ego." The ego is the strongest element so that it can manage this balance. If the id gets too strong, the person starts to act on their own urges without regard to anything else, while if the super-ego becomes too strong, a person becomes controlled by rigid morals, and is perhaps constantly overwhelmed by feelings of guilt. Freud wrote, "Psycho-analysis is an instrument to enable the ego to achieve a progressive conquest of the id."

Conflict between the id and the super-ego may result in anxiety, guilt, and frustration. The ego, struggling to keep the peace between the id and super-ego, may resort to one of the defence mechanisms, such as denial, displacement repression, rationalization, regression, or suppression. These defences are not necessarily unhealthy, but they can be overused, or used inappropriately. Even if repressed by the ego, the desires of the id can continue to affect behavior. Freud considered a balance between the id, ego, and super-ego to be the key to a healthy personality.

Freud's innovative restructuring of the mind opened up new avenues for theories and research, and allowed him to consider different types of mental illness in terms of their origin in a conflict between parts of the personality, or particular defences of the ego. In 1924, he published two papers, "Neurosis and Psychosis," and "The Loss of Reality and Psychosis," which expanded on ideas introduced in *The Ego and the Id*. He considered

transference neurosis to stem from a conflict between ego and id; narcissistic neuroses to stem from a conflict between ego and super-ego; and psychoses to stem from a conflict between ego and the external world.

BELOW *James and Alix Strachey, who undertook the translation of much of Freud's works into English, took part in the 11th International Psycho-Analytical Conference, held in Oxford in 1929.*

IX. Internationaler Psychoanalytischer Kongress

3.—5. September 1925

zu Bad Homburg (bei Frankfurt a. M.)

im Kurhaus daselbst.

—•—

Die Teilnehmer des Kongresses treffen sich am Vorabend (Mittwoch, den 2. September) um 8.30 im genannten Kurhaus zu einem zwanglosen Beisammensein. Bei dieser Gelegenheit werden Mitglieder und Gäste ihre Teilnehmerkarten erhalten.

Für die Verhandlungen des Kongresses hat der Vorstand das umstehende Programm aufgestellt.

Ninth Congress

of the International Psycho-Analytical Association

September 3d—5th 1925

in Bad Homburg (near Frankfurt a. M.)

—•—

The Ninth Congress of the International Psycho-Analytical Association will be held in Bad Homburg at the Kurhaus.

The members and the guests who take part in the Congress will meet on the previous evening (Wednesday, September 2d) at 8.30 p. m. at the Kurhaus.

There they will receive their attendance cards.

The Congress will proceed according to the following Programme.

VORTRÄGE THEORETISCHEN INHALTS
PAPERS ON THEORETICAL QUESTIONS

Donnerstag,
den 3. September
vorm. 9 Uhr

Thursday,
September 3rd.
at 9 a.m.

1. *Dr. K. LANDAUER, Frankfurt a.M.:* Automatisierung und Zwangsneurose.

2. *Dr. T. BURROW, Baltimore:* The Laboratory Method in Psychoanalysis. (Its Inception and Development.)

3. *Dr. I. HERMANN, Budapest:* Regressionen der Ich-Orientierung.

4. *Dr. J. van OPHUIJSEN, Haag:* Some remarks on the Origin of Sadism.

5. *Dr. C. MÜLLER-BRAUNSCHWEIG, Berlin:* Zur Libidotheorie und Strukturanalyse.

VORTRÄGE THERAPEUTISCHEN INHALTS
PAPERS ON THERAPEUTICAL QUESTIONS

Donnerstag,
den 3. September
nachm. 3³⁰ Uhr

Thursday,
September 3rd.
at 3³⁰ p.m.

1. *Dr. S. FERENCZI, Budapest:* Kontraindikationen der aktiven psychoanalytischen Technik.

2. *Dr. E. JONES, London:* The Significance of the alloerotic components of the Super-Ego for Therapie.

3. *Dr. M. I. EISLER, Budapest:* Die Bedeutung der Idealbildungen für die psychoanalytische Therapie.

4. *Dr. F. ALEXANDER, Berlin:* Neurose und Gesamtpersönlichkeit.

5. *Dr. L. P. CLARK, New York:* The Phantasy Method of Analysing Narcissistic Neuroses.

VORTRÄGE KLINISCHEN INHALTS
PAPERS ON CLINICAL MATTERS

Freitag,
den 4. September
vorm. 9 Uhr

Friday,
September 4th.
at 9 a.m.

1. *Dr. I. H. CORIAT, Boston:* The Oral-Erotik Components of Stammering.

2. *Dr. W. REICH, Wien:* Libidostruktur und Genese der hypochondrischen Neurasthenie.

3. *Dr. O. FENICHEL, Berlin:* Zur Klinik des Strafbedürfnisses.

4. *Dr. S. E. JELIFFE, New York:* Organic Desease as Symbolic Castration (Myopia as Illustration).

5. *Dr. S. PFEIFER, Budapest:* Bioanalyse organisch-pathologischer Zustände.

Freitag,
den 4. September
nachm. keine
Verhandlungen

Friday,
September 4th.
Afternoon
No proceedings

VORTRÄGE ÜBER ANGEWANDTE PSYCHOANALYSE
PAPERS ON APPLIED PSYCHO-ANALYSIS

Sonnabend,
den 5. September
vorm. 9 Uhr

Saturday,
September 5th.
at 9 a.m.

1. *Dr. J. VAN EMDEN, Haag:* Zur Bedeutung der Spinne in Symbolik und Folklore.

2. *Dr. G. ROHEIM, Budapest:* The Scapegoat.

3. *Dr. Th. REIK, Wien:* Der Ursprung der Psychologie.

4. *Dr. O. PFISTER, Zürich:* Zur Psychologie der Unduldsamkeit.

5. *Dr. M. D. EDER, London:* A Contribution to the Psychologie of Snobbism.

GESCHÄFTLICHE SITZUNG
BUSINESS MEETING

Sonnabend,
den 5. September
nachm. 3³⁰ Uhr

Saturday,
September 5th.
at 3³⁰ p.m.

1. Berichte des Vorstandes und der Gruppenvorsitzenden.

2. Berichte des Berliner und des Wiener psychoanalytischen Institutes.

3. Bericht des Verlages.

4. Anträge.

5. Präsidentenwahl.

6. Nächster Kongreß.

Am Abend des zweiten Kongreßtages findet ein Bankett der Teilnehmer des Kongresses statt.

Alle sich auf den Kongreß beziehenden Anfragen und Mitteilungen sind bis zum 15. August an den unterzeichneten Zentralsekretär zu richten. Nach dem 15. August wolle man sich in Angelegenheiten der Unterkunft in Bad Homburg an *Herrn Dr. K. LANDAUER, Frankfurt a. M., Kettenhofweg 17,* wenden.

On the evening of the second day of the Congress there will be a banquet for those attending the Congress.

Inquiries about hotel-arrangements and all other matters of the Congress should be adressed to the undersigned General Secretary till to August 15th.

After August 15th. inquiries about hotel-arrangements in Bad Homburg should be adressed to *Dr. K. LANDAUER, Frankfurt a. M., Kettenhofweg 17.*

Dr. Karl ABRAHAM
Präsident

Dr. Max EITINGON
Sekretär

The program for the ninth congress of the IPA, held in 1925 in Homburg. The different categories of papers and the breadth of speakers shows how far the international psychoanalytical movement had come since the early twentieth century. Freud had not attended a congress since 1922, but on this occasion Anna presented a paper written by him for the congress, which was well received.

Life and Death Drives

In 1911, Freud published an important paper, *Formulierungen Über Die Zwei Prinzipien Des Psychischen Geschehens* (*Formulations on the Two Principles of Mental Functioning*). In his book on dreams, he had divided mental processes into primary (regulated by the pleasure principle) and secondary (regulated by the reality principle). This paper looked at how these processes interact.

He explained that the primary processes of the mind, which were originally the only processes, are governed by the pleasure principle. These processes simply strive toward gaining pleasure. Mental

RIGHT *Freud's collection of sculptures includes six figures of Eros, of which this Greek terracotta figure is the largest.*
He identified the basic life/love drive as "Eros."

activity shrinks from any event that might spoil pleasure: for example, repression.

Mental functioning later develops the reality principle. Under the influence of the ego, the pleasure principle is replaced with the reality principle, which does not abandon the pursuit of pleasure, but goes about obtaining it in a realistic way, tolerating lack of pleasure on the way, if necessary. (Freud notes at this point that the religious doctrine of reward in the afterlife following renunciation of early pleasures is simply a mythical projection of the revolution in the mind.) So the ego of a child develops as the child grows in order to better secure happiness in the external world. The pleasure principle sometimes manages to overwhelm the reality principle to the detriment of the person.

After the First World War, death and violence became more prominent in Freud's thinking, so it is perhaps not a surprise that in 1919, he began to revise his theory of the instincts or drives by positing a death instinct in his book *Beyond the Pleasure Principle*. This book contains quite philosophical and speculative ideas and is further removed from his casework than previous publications. Freud put these new ideas forward quite tentatively, admitting that it was speculation, but feeling that was inevitable in the "uncharted terrain" he was now entering. His biographer Ernest Jones noted that Freud had always had quite a speculative nature. When younger, he had always kept it in check, but at this time was allowing it more free rein. This book, dealing with nothing less than the origin of life and the nature of death, was probably his most speculative, and the least accepted by his followers. The complex ideas are difficult to summarize, and have often been misrepresented.

> **❝** *At the moment I am dissatisfied with everything – for no obvious reason.* **❞**

– SIGMUND FREUD

LEFT *Oskar Nemon working on a bust of Sigmund Freud, as Freud stands alongside, in Vienna, 1931.*

Freud thought that a profound conflict must exist within the mind, and wanted to explore what the opposing forces were in this conflict. Previously, he had paired the libidinal and egoistic drives together, but had since begun to question this. He felt sure there must be some instinct in the mind, presumably in the ego, that contrasted more dramatically with the sexual instinct.

Freud returned to the existing principle, noted in his 1911 paper (*Formulations on the Two Principles of Mental Functioning*), that the main aim of mental activity is to reduce the tensions created by external/instinctual excitement, aiming at a position of rest. This fitted with his theory of wish fulfilment, where impulses seek satisfaction (through dreams, for example), then come to rest.

He then considered the human tendency to repeat unpleasurable experiences, overriding the pleasure principle. This was something he had seen in his patients, but he also noted how children repeat games or stories, regardless of whether they are pleasurable. He used the example of his grandson who would hide toys in an enactment of his mother being absent, over and over again. He also discussed how those suffering trauma from their experiences in the First World War tended to re-enact their traumatic experiences. He thought that repeating these unpleasant experiences was done to master or bind them, to become the active rather than passive part of the experience. This process of mastering primitive impressions was necessary before the pleasure principle could operate.

Freud considered that the tendency to repeat can be equated with restoring a previous state of affairs. He therefore concluded that the fundamental aim of all instincts was to revert to an earlier stage, a regression, meaning that they are essentially conservative. The overall aim was to return an organism to a pre-living state – death. So the ultimate aim in life is death. Even the sexual and self-preservation instincts can be seen to fit into this theory, their function being essentially to allow individuals to avoid untimely death, instead allowing them to die in their own fashion. This conclusion didn't work for Freud's theory of combative instincts, however, and he speculated that although the sexual and self-preservation instincts were conservative in nature, their actions had the merit of postponing death, and therefore the ultimate goal of the instincts. Also that in creating new life, they could be said to be opposing the aim of the death instinct.

Freud had now formulated the conflict he felt had to be present in the mind: He combined the instincts for self-preservation and preservation of the species under the concept of "Eros," the life/love drive. He contrasted this drive with a death or destructive drive, which a follower of Freud later named "Thanatos."

The Eros instinct fosters pro-social actions and cooperation. Energy created by Thanatos can be expressed toward the self, as self-destructive behavior, or outward toward others, as aggression and violence. Freud suggested that masochism was a self-injuring tendency arising from the death drive, and sadistic impulses were derived from this. The complexities of life arise from the interplay of Eros and Thanatos, which create a paradox which cannot be fully resolved. This interaction could explain much about the forces that shape the behavior of both individuals and societies. Freud's idea was that in the struggle of the Eros instinct to delay the fulfilment of the Thanatos drive, self-destructive tendencies were diverted outward, toward other people, similar to how a ruler might redirect a revolutionary impulse in his country by bringing about war with another country.

Freud's preoccupation with death, in *Beyond the Pleasure Principle* and other works, has invited many to regard this as a consequence of his grief over his daughter's death. However, much of the work on this book was completed well before she died.

Hilda Doolittle (1886–1961)

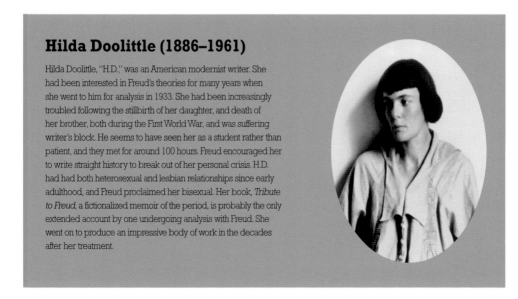

Hilda Doolittle, "H.D.," was an American modernist writer. She had been interested in Freud's theories for many years when she went to him for analysis in 1933. She had been increasingly troubled following the stillbirth of her daughter, and death of her brother, both during the First World War, and was suffering writer's block. He seems to have seen her as a student rather than patient, and they met for around 100 hours. Freud encouraged her to write straight history to break out of her personal crisis. H.D. had had both heterosexual and lesbian relationships since early adulthood, and Freud proclaimed her bisexual. Her book, *Tribute to Freud*, a fictionalized memoir of the period, is probably the only extended account by one undergoing analysis with Freud. She went on to produce an impressive body of work in the decades after her treatment.

It may, however, be questioned whether he would have pursued such a train of thought before the First World War.

Freud was very tentative about his conclusions in *Beyond the Pleasure Principle*, though he would build upon these foundations in *The Ego and the Id*, and further developed the themes in *Civilization and its Discontents*, published in 1930. Even in the latter book he acknowledged that the existence of the death drive was open to debate, but by that time it had become indispensable to his way of thinking. The theories met with a very mixed reception among analysts, and were accepted by only a few.

At the same time as *Beyond the Pleasure Principle*, Freud was working on *Group Psychology and Analysis of the Ego*. In this book he put forward a theory that individual and social psychology were essentially the same. He then applied his life and death instincts to the dynamics of large groups, looking at why people follow leaders and why they deny some of their desires to live together.

Freud would explore society and why/how people suppressed their instincts to live in society in one of his most widely read books, *Das Unbehagen in der Kultur* (*Civilization and its Discontents*) – the German title translates as The Uneasiness in Culture, which perhaps is closer to expressing the main theme. This work is an example of how Freud's interests and writings grew wider in his later years, returning to topics of cultural, social, and philosophical issues that had interested him in his youth.

Freud was interested in the fundamental tensions between the individual and civilization. He saw a paradox in the fact that humans created civilization to protect themselves from unhappiness, and yet it is the largest source of unhappiness to humans. Freud noted three main sources of suffering which people attempt to master: their own bodies, "doomed to decay and dissolution and which cannot even do without pain and anxiety as warning signals"; the cruel and destructive aspects of the natural world; and finally, relations with other men – the suffering inevitably caused by having to live with others in a society. He considered that this last was the most painful source of displeasure that a person would have to contemplate.

This is because all humans are controlled by the life and death drives, but the satisfaction of their desires is necessarily frustrated by living in society. Although society may have been formulated to satisfy the pleasure principle, it has to make compromises of happiness in order to fulfil the primary goal of bringing people together into peaceful harmony, which is done by making them subject to a higher authority.

Freud discussed the origins of society, combining his ideas with Darwinian theories on the earliest humans, and borrowing ideas from anthropology, some of which were already discredited when he adopted them. In a previous book, *Totem und Tabu* (Totem and Taboo), Freud had presented a hypothetical scenario where a group of brothers who had been driven out of the primal horde returned and killed and devoured their father, whom they both feared and respected. Their guilt at this Oedipal murder then caused them to set up certain taboos (in fact, a delayed obedience to their father's will) by which early society lived. Freud saw this as the beginning of human morality in the earliest stages of society, as well as religion and social life.

Society's laws forbid certain behaviors, such as rape, killing, incest, and adultery, and formulate punishments for them. Because these constrain the desires of individuals, civilization inevitably provokes feelings of discontent among its members.

While an individual's Eros instinct can work toward the purpose of society, the drive for death and destruction has to be either repressed, or directed against a rival culture. Freud noted that when an individual's impulses are denied direct sexual or aggressive satisfaction, they can be channelled into other areas, such as religion, art, and science. Therefore, civilization, as life, is borne out of the struggle between the drives of life/love and death/destruction.

For Freud, the vital questions were about the consequences for the individual if society did not

Sándor Ferenczi (1873–1933)

Ferenczi was for many years close to Freud, but the Rank affair in the 1920s was the start of their separation. The increasing distance between them in subsequent years saddened Freud. In the late 20s, Ferenczi began to develop theories divergent from psychoanalysis, returning to Freud's early abandoned theory of sexual abuse in childhood causing neurosis. He also developed different therapeutic techniques, aiming to act as a loving parent to neutralize the early unhappiness of his patients, and allowing his patients to kiss him. Freud strongly disagreed with this. The two clashed verbally, meeting for the last time in 1932, though they remained on outwardly friendly terms after this. Ferenczi died from pernicious anaemia in 1933.

only fantasized about. This guilt is the price paid for being part of society, and is unconscious guilt that is experienced by the individual as anxiety or "discontent."

Freud felt that civilization was vulnerable to radical disruption, stemming as it did from unresolvable conflicts. He had already seen many violent social crises in his own country and in Europe during his lifetime. He fitted these into his model of psychological conflict as symptoms of the primal conflicts of society. In his theories, he emphasized how participation in mass society released deep-seated aggressive impulses. Crises in society reveal aspects of human nature that are hidden in normal day-to-day living.

Freud described *Civilization and its Discontents* to Lou Andreas-Salomé thus: "It deals with civilization, consciousness of guilt, happiness and similar lofty matters." The book was his fullest account of his views on sociology, and although he himself was not that satisfied with it, it sold well.

But Freud's theories would not protect him from the fallout of another "violent social crisis" – the rise of the Nazis to power in Germany during the early 1930s, and their subsequent annexation of Austria in 1938.

satisfy their desires, and also the consequences for society. He found no way out of the dilemma, noting how some individuals become neurotic through their repression of the death instinct, and how all individuals feel guilt as a consequence of being part of society. This is because the super-ego punishes the ego not only for things the individual has done (remorse), but also for sins that the individual has

ABOVE *Portrait of Freud by H. Frank, completed around 1935.*

LEFT *Freud and Marie Bonaparte in his study in 1937.*

Escape from Nazism

The early 1930s saw Freud continue to struggle with cancer. Until 1931, it was hoped that the first radical operations in 1923 had led to a permanent cure, but when it was discovered that yet another "suspicious" place removed during surgery had been on the point of becoming malignant, that hope was extinguished. From then on it was simply a case of treating recurrences as early as possible. The year 1932 was a bad year, during which Freud underwent five operations. He was only able to travel to the suburbs of Vienna for his summer holiday in 1931. In fact, he did not leave Vienna again until he was forced to in 1938. His mother died in 1930, an event about which he wrote: "No pain, no grief, which is probably to be explained

by the circumstances, the great age and the end of the pity we had felt at her helplessness. With that a feeling of liberation … I was not allowed to die as long as she was alive, and now I may."

The world economic crisis of the early 1930s was causing analysts in all countries economic problems, and the 1931 congress was postponed as so few would have been able to afford to attend. The trickle of psychoanalysts emigrating to America soon became a steady stream.

Freud's earnings diminished, and then his practice also began to shrink, about which he wrote: "I am too old, and working with me is too precarious. I should not need to work any longer." Owing to the economic crisis, his book sales reduced, which made the continued existence of the Verlag (see Chapter 13) even more perilous than previously, depending as it did on the continued revenue stream from the sale of Freud's works. In 1931, Freud's son Martin gave up his job to take on the Verlag, managing to come to terms with all the Verlag's creditors, and Freud had to make an appeal to the IPA to take responsibility for the Verlag in the future. Most of the societies offered immediate help, and at the 1932 congress all members became obligated to subscribe three dollars a month for at least two years to maintain the Verlag. The political consequences of the world economic crisis, however, would soon overshadow the economic implications, particularly in Germany and Austria.

Adolf Hitler (1889–1945) became Chancellor of Germany in January 1933, and in April, a nation-wide "Action against the Un-German Spirit" was launched by the National Socialist German Students' Association. The launch climaxed in

ABOVE *Freud on the balcony of his summer home in 1935.*

a book-burning, where over 25,000 "un-German" books were symbolically burned on the night of May 10 by university students. The largest event was in Berlin, where 40,000 people threw books into the flames after a rousing address by Joseph Goebbels (1897–1945). The books burnt that night included those written by Karl Marx (1818–1883) and Vladimir Ilyich Lenin (1870–1924); Nobel-Prize winning German author Thomas Mann (1875–1955); well-known socialists such as Bertolt Brecht (1898–1956); bourgeois writers; "corrupting foreign influences" such as Ernest Hemingway (1899–1961) and H. G. Wells (1866–1946); and inevitably, works by notable Jewish authors including the beloved nineteenth-century poet Heinrich Heine (1797–1856), Franz Werfel (1890–1945), Max Brod (1884–1968), Stefan Zweig (1881–1942), and Freud himself. As well as Freud's work, many other psychoanalytical books were burnt in the fires – psychoanalysis was on the Nazi blacklist. Freud commented on the events: "What progress we are making. In the Middle Ages they would have burnt me; nowadays they are content with burning my books." Others took it more seriously, urging him to flee Austria while there was still time.

Another great mind whose books were burned that night in Berlin was Albert Einstein (1879–1955), the Nobel-Prize winning physicist. Freud and Einstein had met in Berlin in 1927. Einstein did not believe in psychoanalysis, but the two got on well by avoiding their professional fields and discussing politics. In 1931, Einstein was invited by the Institute for Intellectual Co-operation (who were asked to do so by the League of Nations) to exchange ideas with a thinker of his choice, with the results to be published. He chose to discuss whether there was any way of delivering mankind from war, and to help him fathom this question, he chose Freud, with his insights into the human mind. Both abhorred war, Freud describing it as "futile" in his letter to Einstein. In his letter to Freud, Einstein suggested an international legislative and judicial organization that would settle disputes between nations. All nations would surrender some of their sovereignty and agree to abide by the decisions of the international organization, in the interests of security, a suggestion that Freud agreed with.

Freud took a couple of months to compose his reply, and feared that his thoughts on the matter

Burning knowledge

Shortly after coming to power, the Nazis began to bring Germany into line with their ideology, and Joseph Goebbels started an offensive on non-German arts and culture. Goebbels found an ally in the National Socialist German Students' Association, and in April 1933 an "Action" against the Un-German "Spirit," described as an affirmation of traditional German values, and a response to a worldwide Jewish "smear campaign" against Germany began. The climatic event of this "action" was a literary purge by fire, a *Säuberung*. In most university towns, right-wing students marched in parades by torchlight, then after listening to speeches, they threw thousands of books onto bonfires with much ceremony. Naturally, the books included many by Jewish authors, such as those of Sigmund Freud.

would not be very encouraging, worrying that the Institute might not even wish to publish his pessimistic text. In his reply to Einstein, Freud outlined his theory of the life/love and death/hate instincts. Since aggression is a manifestation of Thanatos (see Chapter 15), it is essential to human nature and there is "no likelihood of our being able to suppress humanity's aggressive tendencies." As aggression cannot be suppressed, it should be diverted into a channel other than that of war. He therefore suggested indirect ways of combating war by introducing Eros (see Chapter 15) into the equation: education to create independent minds; fostering a sense of identification to create a community of feeling. Freud concluded his reply with the hope that in time cultural attitudes and a dread of the consequences of a future war might put an end to war itself as other men become pacifists, as he and Einstein were.

Rather than being disappointed with the reply, Einstein was delighted with Freud's writing. The correspondence was collected in a small book called *Warum Krieg* (*Why War?*), which was published in German, French, and English just after Hitler came to power in 1933. Freud commented in a letter that it could be neither advertised nor sold in Germany. After the book burnings and the passing of a law to bar Jews holding any official positions, including teaching at universities, Einstein emigrated to America in 1933, along with many other German scientists.

The ruling that no Jews were to serve on any scientific council in 1933 meant that Max Eitingon (see Chapter 12) was replaced as president of the German Psychoanalytic Association, though Freud was sure this would not prevent the eventual banning of psychoanalysis in Germany. In June the German Society for Psychotherapy came under Nazi control and was restructured as the International General Medical Society for Psychotherapy, with Carl Jung (see chapter 12) as president. All members were expected to study Hitler's *Mein Kampf* (*My Struggle*) and use it as a basis for their work. Jewish emigration from Germany was now in full swing and 1934 saw the last Jewish analysts leaving the country.

LEFT *Hitler's car surrounded by cheering crowds in Vienna in March 1938.*

At the very end of 1933, Eitingon emigrated to Palestine, leaving Ernest Jones as the only remaining member of the committee in Europe. The German Society was made to withdraw from membership of the IPA in 1936. By then, training analyses in Germany were forbidden; lectures were still allowed, but were all attended by Nazis to ensure that no technical terms were used. The Leipzig property of the Verlag (see Chapter 13) was seized in 1936, and the publishing programme for Germany had to be cancelled. When German psychoanalyst Felix Boehm (1881–1958) managed to visit Freud in 1937 to tell him what was going on in Germany, Freud was furious.

Freud had painful radiation treatment in 1934, and two operations in 1935. While he continued to bear the pain stoically, his letters reveal a growing feeling that as he approached 80, he had nothing left to give or look forward to. He also considered that now he no longer smoked, he was only likely to write letters. Sándor Ferenczi (see Chapter 12) died in May 1933, and Freud wrote to Jones, "Our loss is great and painful ... Ferenczi takes with him a part of the old time; then with my departure another will begin... ." He was no longer worried for the future of psychoanalysis, but only for the future of his children and grandchildren.

In 1935, Freud was delighted to be made an honorary member of the Royal Society of Medicine. In 1936, he turned 80, and celebrated his golden wedding anniversary, both as quietly as possible. Congratulations poured in from around the world, and Freud spent weeks struggling to acknowledge them all. However, a few weeks after his eightieth birthday, he wrote to Stefan Zweig (1881–1942): "Although I have been exceptionally happy in my home, with my wife and children ... I nevertheless cannot reconcile myself to the wretchedness and helplessness of old age, and look forward with a kind of longing to the transition into non-existence." In late 1936, he wrote to Marie Bonaparte: "... tortured as I am by the conflict between the desire for rest, the dread of renewed suffering ..., and by the anticipation of sorrow at being separated from everything to which I am still attached." In July 1936, Freud had two more operations, and for the first time since 1923, cancer was found. He had further operations in late 1936, and 1937.

Hitler himself was Austrian, and a National Socialist movement had been formed in Austria at the beginning of the twentieth century, so it was not long before concerted efforts were made to bring Austria into the Nazi fold. Unification had been favored by many Germans and Austrians for a number of years, but had been prohibited after the First World War to limit Germany's strength. An attempted coup by Austrian and German Nazis in 1934, of which Freud wrote, "our little bit of civil war was not at all nice," was unsuccessful, but in March 1938, Austria was occupied and annexed by Nazi Germany. The right-wing chancellor had been forced to resign after Hitler had insisted that Nazis be admitted to his cabinet, and his pro-Nazi replacement invited German troops into the country to restore law and order. Austria had become part of the Greater German Reich.

Many Austrians were approving of and even enthusiastic for the Anschluss, but liberal, left-wing and Jewish Austrians had legitimate concerns for the future. Freud had expected the Nazis to eventually take over Austria, and had previously commented that he hoped not to live to see it, as he knew that he and his family would most probably have to leave their home. In 1938, Austria had a Jewish population of around 192,000 – almost 4 percent of the population – and the majority of them lived in Vienna. Almost immediately, German anti-Jewish legislation was extended to Austria, restricting rights, freedom of movement, education, and work options. Arrests and public humiliation of Jews were soon very common. Later in the year Mauthausen concentration camp would be built in Austria, and that November saw *Kristallnacht*, a wave of violent anti-Jewish pogroms.

Freud was now in his 80s, and frail. He had debated leaving Vienna for a foreign land many

ABOVE *19 Berggasse, Vienna, after the Anschluss.*

take him, and finally, that he could not leave his home country. He eventually agreed that Jones should try and get permission for him to go to his beloved England. In agreeing to go, Freud seems to have been thinking mainly of Anna's future. In several letters he comments that emigrating "for us old people" would not have been worthwhile, but that the upheaval was worth it for her sake.

Freud had loved England since he was a boy, and had always envied his half-brothers for moving there and raising their children free from the anti-Semitism he had experienced in Austria. His subsequent trips there had reinforced his love of the country and its culture. His youngest son Ernst had emigrated to London with his family in 1933 after the rise of the Nazis. When it looked more likely that they would be allowed to leave, Freud wrote to Ernst expressing concern at how he, Martha, and Minna would settle in London, and requesting that he help them in this.

Jones returned to London to try and obtain permission. He received a letter from Sir William Bragg, president of the Royal Society, to the Home

times before, and he fully realized the threat of the Nazi occupation, but was understandably reluctant to leave his home, his possessions and his medical treatment. The Vienna Society decided on March 13, 1938, that all members should flee if they could, with the Society being reestablished wherever Freud settled. The only non-Jewish member of the Society, Richard Sterba (1898–1989), also fled, ignoring requests that he return to take over the Vienna Institute and Clinic. The Germans had no society to take over, instead seizing its library, and confiscating the Verlag (see Chapter 13).

On March 15, around the time the Verlag was filling with soldiers, and Freud's son Martin was placed under arrest, storm troopers visited Freud's house. Martha and Anna had given them all the household money and contents of the safe, in hopes of sending them on their way, and they were debating their next move when Freud appeared, looking furious, and the soldiers hurriedly left.

Knowing how Freud felt about leaving Vienna, Ernest Jones flew to Vienna on March 15, at great personal risk, and arrived just after the departure of the soldiers. He tried to persuade Freud to leave Vienna. Freud protested he did not want to, that he was too weak to travel, and that no country would

ABOVE *Ernst's three sons – Stephen, Lucian, and Clemens (later, Anglicised to Clement) – around 1933, when the family moved from Berlin to London after the Nazis came to power. Freud's other Berlin-based son, Oliver, also left the country in 1933.*

Secretary. The Home Secretary, Sir Samuel Hoare, then gave Jones permission to fill in permits for Freud, his family, servants, his doctor, and some of his pupils with their families. Freud would also aid Joseph Breuer's widow and her family to leave Vienna.

It was not enough, however, to have permission to enter England. The Freuds also needed permission from the Nazis to leave. Luckily, over his long life Freud had made friends in many places, and he now called in favors to help him. The result was that the American chargé d'affaires in Vienna, instructed by the U.S. Secretary of State, worked on the authorities; while the American Ambassador in Paris persuaded the German Ambassador there to speak to the highest authorities he could to ensure Freud was not mistreated; even Mussolini's ambassador in Vienna weighed in on Freud's behalf. Even so, it took three months of anxious waiting before he was granted exit permits.

A week after the initial raid on the Freud home, the Gestapo came and searched his home, but not Freud's rooms, looking for political anti-Nazi documents. They took Anna away with them, detaining her for the whole day, and interrogating her. Freud was beside himself with fear for his beloved daughter, upon whom he was so dependent. Anna would spend much of her time over the next few months dealing with the authorities and arrangements to leave not only on her parents' behalf, but also for others, mainly other psychoanalysts and their families.

Before Jones had left Vienna, Marie Bonaparte arrived to support the Freuds. During the long wait for permits, she and Anna sorted Freud's papers, the results of decades of prodigious writing and correspondence, putting some aside to take to London, and burning the rest. Freud selected the books he wished to take, and the rest were sold. To fill the time, he read about London, undertook translation work for the first time in many years, and continued with his extensive correspondence. He took several drives through Vienna to say farewell to the city he had both loved and hated for so much

of his life. In late May he observed in a letter to Minna, "Everything is in a certain sense unreal, we are no longer here and not yet there."

Copies of Freud's 12-volume *Gesammelte Schriften* (*Complete Works*, published in 1924, 1925, 1928 and 1934) – secreted in Switzerland by Martin Freud – were ordered to be brought back, then confiscated and burned. Martin Freud himself was regularly questioned by the Gestapo.

Before granting the exit permit, the authorities demanded huge sums of money from Freud under the guise of income tax and/or so-called "fugitive tax." Freud could not afford to pay, and the Nazis threatened to take his library and collection of antiquities. Marie Bonaparte managed to sort out the problem for them. The contents of Freud's bank account were confiscated, though he did have some money saved outside of Austria. He had also preserved some funds in gold, following his experience of losing all his savings after the First World War. These Marie Bonaparte managed to smuggle out of the country to London, via the King of Greece.

The authorities also insisted that before he receive an exit permit, Freud sign a statement that he had been treated with respect by the Gestapo and German authorities, and allowed to live in full freedom, with no complaints. He is said to have responded by asking if he could add the sentence, "I can most highly recommend the Gestapo to anyone."

In early May, Minna, seriously ill and nearly blind, was the first to be given permission to leave. Anna's close friend Dorothy Burlingham (1891–1979) collected her from the sanatorium and escorted her to London. Martin Freud, and Mathilde and Robert Hollitscher, were given permission to leave before their parents. Martin's family had already gone to Paris. The youngest of Freud's siblings, Alexander, also successfully escaped from Vienna in 1938. Finally, Freud received his permit and documents, and on June 4, he left Vienna, his home for 79 years.

Der 80. Geburtstag Sigmund Freud's sei uns willkommener An-
lass, um dem Initiator eines neuen und tieferen Wissens vom Men-
schen unseren Glückwunsch und unsere Ehrfurcht auszusprechen.
In jeder Sphäre seines Wirkens bedeutend, als Arzt und Psycho-
loge, als Philosoph und Künstler, ist dieser mutige Erkenner und
Heiler ein Wegweiser für zwei Generationen gewesen in bis-
her ungeahnte Welten der menschlichen Seele. Ein ganz auf sich
selbst gestellter Geist , ein "Mann und Ritter mit erzenem
Blick", wie Nietzsche von Schopenhauer sagt, ein Denker und For-
scher, der allein zu stehen wusste und dann freilich viele an
sich und mit sich zog, ist er seinen Weg gegangen und zu Wahr-
heiten vorgestossen, die deshalb gefährlich erschienen, weil
sie angeblich Verdecktes enthüllten und Dunkelheiten erleuch-
teten. Allerorts legte er neue Probleme frei und änderte die al-
ten Masse; er hat im Suchen und Finden den Raum der geistigen
Forschung vervielfacht und auch seine Gegner sich verpflichtet
durch den schöpferischen Antrieb, den sie von ihm erfuhren. Mögen
künftige Zeiten dies oder jenes Ergebnis seiter Forschung mo-
deln und einschränken- nie mehr sind die Fragen, die Sigmund
Freud der Menschheit gestellt hat, zum Schweigen zu bringen ,
seine Erkenntnisse können nicht dauernd verneint oder getrübt
werden. Die Begriffe, die er gestaltet, die Worte, die er für
sie wählt, sind schon als selbstverständlich eingegangen in die
lebendige Sprache ; auf allen Gebieten der Geisteswissenschaft,
in Literatur- und Kunstforschung , Religionsgeschichte und Prä-
historie, Mythologie, Volkskunde und Pädagogik, nicht zuletzt in
der Dichtung selbst ist die tiefe Spur seines Wirkens zu sehen,
und wenn eine Tat unseres Geschlechtes, so wird, wie sind des-
sen gewiss, seine Erkenntnistat der Seelenkunde unvergesslich
bleiben.
Wir Unterzeichneten, die wir Freud's kühnes Lebenswerk aus un-
serer geistigen Welt nicht wegzudenken vermögen, sind glücklich,
diesen grossen Unermüdlichen unter uns zu wissen und mit unge-
brochener Kraft am Werke zu sehen. Möge unser denkbares Empfinden
den verehrten Mann noch lange begleiten dürfen.

Virginia Woolf   Jules Romains   Romain Rolland   Thomas Mann   Stefan Zweig

On the occasion of Freud's 80th birthday, Thomas Mann visited him at his home and
presented him with a congratulatory address, signed by no fewer than 191 writers and
artists. Visible on this page are those signatures of Virginia Woolf, Jules Romains, Romain
Rolland, H. G. Wells, and Stefan Zweig. Others included James Joyce, Pablo Picasso,
Salvador Dalí, and Aldous Huxley.

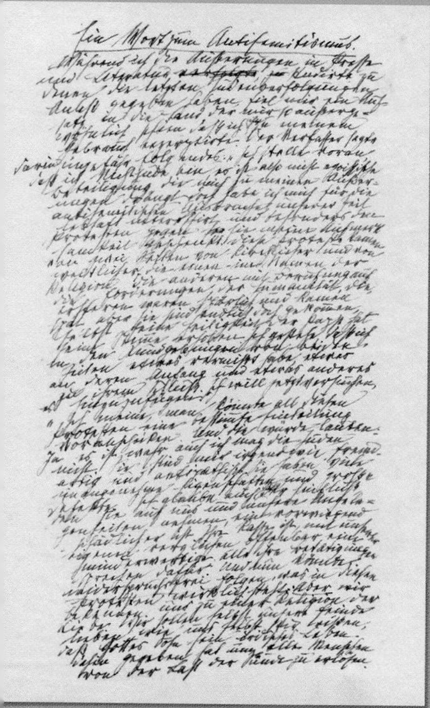

Ein Wort zum Antisemitismus.

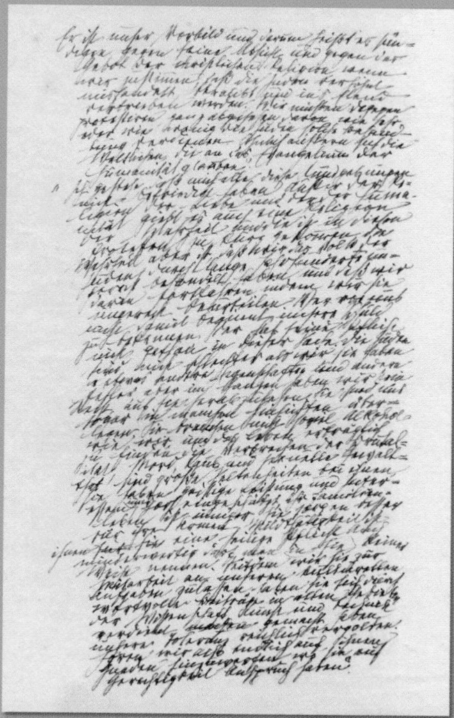

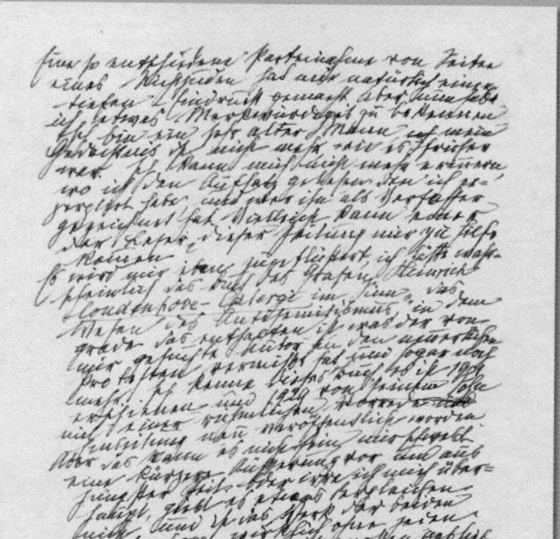

Sigm. Freud

An essay Freud wrote entitled "A Word about Anti-Semitism" which appeared in the magazine *Die Zukunft* (*The Future*) on November 25, 1938.

Exile in London

On his journey out of post-Anschluss Austria, Freud was accompanied by Martha, Anna, two maidservants and his beloved chow, Lün. His doctor Max Schur could not travel with them because of an appendicitis, so another doctor, who was a friend of Anna's, came with them instead.

They left Vienna on June 4, 1938, and travelled to Paris on the Orient Express. They were met by Marie Bonaparte, Ambassador Bullitt (1891–1967)

who had done so much to ensure Freud's good treatment in Vienna – and Harry and Ernst Freud. A number of journalists and photographers also met the train at the station. After a few hours' rest at Marie Bonaparte's home, they crossed to Dover on the ferry. The final leg of the journey was by train, and the Lord Privy Seal arranged that their train arrive at another platform at Victoria than the usual one, so Freud could avoid the huge crowds

> **"** *With ever less regret do I wait for the curtain to fall for me.* **"**

– SIGMUND FREUD

of cameras and well-wishers gathered to see him. Waiting for the train were Martin, Mathilde, and Ernest Jones. Jones drove the family immediately to their temporary home, 39 Elsworthy Road, in north London. The journey had been a strain on an elderly and sick man, but Freud was soon able to enjoy the garden, with its views of London – a welcome change from his emptying flat in tension-filled Vienna.

OPPOSITE *Freud arriving in France, accompanied by Anna, Marie Bonaparte, and her son, Prince Peter of Greece.*

ABOVE *Resting in Marie Bonaparte's garden in Saint-Cloud, before leaving for London the same evening, June 5, 1938. From left: Anna, Freud, Martha, Ernst.*

ABOVE *20 Maresfield Gardens, Hampstead, London –*
Freud's last home.

Freud was pleased by the big welcome he received
in London – not only both the public expressions
of pleasure at his safe arrival, demonstrated in the
newspapers and medical journals and the huge
crowds that had gathered at Victoria, but also the
private gestures seen in the stream of flowers, gifts,
and letters sent to the family, many from strangers,
over the coming weeks. The same month that Freud
arrived, he received three secretaries of the Royal
Society, who brought the official charter book to
Freud for him to sign. The only person to have
previously been honored in this way was the King
himself. He was also delighted to be given a copy of
the book, in which he found himself in the company
of Darwin and Isaac Newton. Freud wrote to his
brother: "In short, for the first time and late in life
I have experienced what it is to be famous."

However, Freud still mourned for his beloved
"prison" Vienna. A few months after the move
he admitted that everything was "rather strange,
difficult and often bewildering." He also missed
his dog and constant companion, Lün, who had
been placed in quarantine for six months. His
sister-in-law Minna was still gravely ill, and he was
too weak to climb the stairs to visit her sickroom
on the first floor. Freud had also had to leave his
four sisters, Dolfi, Mitzi, Rosa, and Pauli, behind
in Vienna. He and his brother Alexander had
given them a sum of money sufficient to live on,
so long as the Nazis did not confiscate it. Initially,
Freud was not overly anxious about their safety,
but each time events progressed in Germany, he
would worry afresh. Marie Bonaparte attempted
to get them permission to leave Austria, but was
unsuccessful. Fortunately for Freud, he did not
live long enough to see the full extent of the
Holocaust. Despite being old ladies in their 70s

and 80s, Freud's sisters were not safe, and none of them survived the war. Dolfi died in Theresienstadt, and the other three were all murdered in Treblinka.

The family moved to a hotel in September, while their permanent home at 20 Maresfield Gardens was prepared for them. However, a few days after arriving, Freud had to undergo another operation, and was transferred to a clinic, where Hans Pichler performed the surgery, having come from Vienna just to do it. It was the most serious operation since the first in 1923, and he never fully recovered from it, becoming increasingly frail. He wrote to Marie Bonaparte on October 4, "I can hardly write, no better than I can speak or smoke."

He finally moved into his last home at the end of September 1938. His son Ernst had redesigned parts of the house for Freud, and arranged his study for him. French windows in the study opened onto the garden, which delighted him. The possessions the family had chosen to bring from Vienna had arrived in August, and all the antiquities and other objects had been arranged on Freud's desk just as they had been in Vienna, so he would immediately feel at home. Ernst also designed a loggia on the back of the house that provided a sheltered area in the garden. Freud was very pleased with the house and garden and spent a lot of time in the garden. The household at Maresfield Gardens consisted of Freud himself, Martha, Minna, and Anna, as well as Anna's friend Dorothy Burlingham and Paula Fichtl, the family's housekeeper.

BELOW *Bookshelves in Freud's study at 20 Maresfield Gardens, with photographs and antiquities arranged as during his lifetime.*

ABOVE *Freud at his desk at his temporary accommodation in Elsworthy Road.*

As he settled in, visitors streamed in to see him. Freud's list of visitors in his dark blue notebook includes over 100 names, and that is not a complete list of everyone who visited him in London during the last 16 months of his life. Many old acquaintances made their way to see Freud, including Max Eitingon, Hanns Sachs, and Ernest Jones, and also members of the British psychoanalytic community, including Joan Riviere, Melanie Klein, and Edward Glover (1888–1972). Other visitors included writers, such as H. G. Wells, Arnold Zweig (1887–1968), and Stefan Zweig. He was also visited by Chaim Weizmann (1874–1952), the Zionist leader. The constant visitors may often have caused Freud pain rather than pleasure, as he was now deaf in one ear, hardly able to talk, and was weak and easily tired too.

Following a dispute between European and American analysts on the question of lay analysis at the Paris Congress of 1938, the European Committee met twice at Freud's house, even though the second time, in late July 1939, he was too ill to contribute much. In November 1938, he received the committee of the Yiddish Scientific Institute, speaking to them about his work on *Der Mann Moses und die monotheistische Religion* (*Moses and Monotheism*), and about the warnings not to publish it that he had received from Jewish sources. By the end of 1938, Freud was able to conduct four analyses daily from his new home, and was continuing on *Abriß der Psychoanalyse* (*An Outline of Psychoanalysis*), more to fill his spare time than to publish.

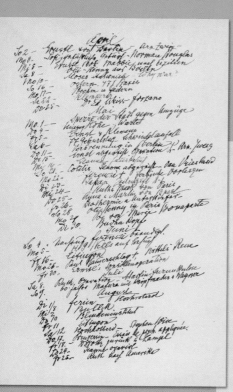

Freud kept an abbreviated personal diary, known as the *Kürzeste Chronik*,
meaning "short chronicle." Included here are pages from 1933 and 1938.
(See Translations on page 154).

Freud and Religion

In his autobiographical study of 1924 Sigmund Freud stated, "My parents were Jews and I have remained a Jew myself." The following year he wrote: "My language is German. My culture, my attainments are German. I considered myself German intellectually, until I noticed the growth of anti-Semitic prejudice in Germany and German Austria. Since that time, I prefer to call myself a Jew." But he observed to his friend, Lutheran pastor Oskar Pfister, that he was a "godless Jew." He also felt that only a "godless Jew" like himself could have discovered the secrets of psychoanalysis. Freud described his family as largely non-observant Jews,

and he himself as an atheist, an unbeliever. In his last year of life he wrote: "Neither in my private life nor in my writings have I ever made a secret of my being an out-and-out unbeliever." However, it was not so clear cut, as although he said his family were non-observant, his father was a devoted student of the Torah, respected for his mastery of biblical texts in Hebrew, and well-versed in Jewish traditions and customs. As a child, therefore, Freud was exposed to his father's close and extensive study of the Bible. So his declaration in later life that his father had let him grow up with no knowledge of Judaism must be at the very least a misremembering, if not a conscious denial of his background. There are suggestions that Freud's rejection of religious Judaism derived from his rejection of his father.

Freud himself studied the Hebrew language and the Bible for six years as a child, and remained on good terms with his teacher, Samuel Hammerschlag (1826–1904), although on occasion he denied any knowledge of Hebrew. He admitted to being deeply engrossed with the Bible as soon as he could read. His father later gave him the prized family Bible, inscribed to his son in Hebrew for his 35th birthday, indicating that Jakob clearly thought his son could still read Hebrew. After Freud's death, his library was found to contain a bible in Hebrew and German, with copious notes added by Freud. Freud said he

LEFT *Print of Moses by Kreuger based on a Rembrandt painting. It hung in Freud's study as a reminder of his last publication,* Moses and Monotheism.

OPPOSITE *Freud working in his study in 1938. He would finish his last published work,* Moses and Monotheism, *in England.*

admired the philosopher Baruch Spinoza (1632–1677), who said that the Bible should be read as critically as any other book; he regarded it as a great book of the Western literary tradition, but nothing more. References to the Bible in Freud's writing are similar to his references to other literary sources.

Although Freud remained a declared unbeliever his whole life, he never denied that he was a Jew, and he embraced the cultural and social side of his Jewish heritage. In fact, "Jewishness" was a preoccupation throughout his life. While studying at university, and throughout his time connected to the university, he was often made to feel inferior because he was Jewish, and his academic progression was halted because he was a Jew. Yet despite this, during his intellectual isolation of the 1890s, he turned to the Jewish club, the B'nai B'rith Society in Vienna, for social activity and remained a member for the rest of his life. He attended social and cultural activities there every other Tuesday and occasionally lectured there.

As a psychoanalyst, he was interested in explaining and dissecting religious belief, as shown by his comments on his patients' mentions of religion in their case histories. He felt that only an unbeliever could understand belief. He considered that reason was making inroads against superstition, but that there was still a long way to go. He saw himself as a solider in the front line of the battle against religion. It has been suggested that his feelings stem from when his nanny, who had introduced him to Catholicism and taken him to church on a regular basis, was made to leave suddenly when he was still a small child (see Chapter 2). He would have had an unconscious need to reject everything she stood for. It has also been noted by his critics that Freud was only interested in the "masses" and their simple religion, and it has been suggested that this was because this simple religion, as shown to the young Freud by his nanny, was the only religion that mattered to him.

In his writings, Freud portrays religion as a primitive attempt to deal with the reality of a frightening world, and the impossibility of satisfying one's fundamental desires. From the mid-1890s onwards, he was interested in constructing a psychology for all of human nature, not just those with neuroses. While his first attempt, the *Project* of 1895, was unfinished and unpublished, he would widen his scope of interests to include the whole range of culture, including religion, which he addressed in his writings several times.

In 1907, Freud wrote *Obsessive Actions and Religious Practices*, which looked at the similarities between the obsessive actions by sufferers of nervous illnesses, and the religious rituals in which believers "give expression to their piety." He saw obsessional neurosis as a type of distorted private religion, and religion as a type of universal obsessional neurosis.

In *Totem and Taboo*, published in 1913, Freud offered an interpretation of the origins of religious ritual, relating it to the Oedipus complex. In 1921, one of the groups that he looked at in *Group Psychology and the Analysis of the Ego* was the Church.

His most detailed examination of religion was *Die Zukunft einer Illusion* (*The Future of an Illusion*), published in 1927, an ambitious exploration of culture, and a statement of his "unbeliefs," an expression of his philosophy rather than an argument based on psychoanalysis. He opened by examining religious ideas, which he calls "perhaps the most important item in the psychical inventory of a civilization." He explained that religious ideas arise from the same needs as all other achievements of civilization – to protect against the superior power of nature. Man needs religion to make his helplessness tolerable. So Freud suggested that the gods retain a threefold task: to exorcise the terrors of nature; reconcile man to the cruelty of Fate; and compensate man for the suffering that living in a civilized society has imposed upon him.

BELOW *The Virgin and Child with Saint Anne by Leonardo da Vinci. Freud performed a psychoanalytic reading of him in his essay "Leonardo da Vinci: A Memory of His Childhood."*

OPPOSITE *Statue of Egyptian Pharoah Amenhotep IV (Akhenaten), of the Eighteenth Dynasty. Akhenaten abandoned Egyptian polytheism and introduced a new form of worship, described as monotheistic. Freud argued that Moses was a follower of Akhenaten, forced to leave Egypt after Akhenaten's death and the reversal of his religious policies, or Akhenaten himself.*

❝ *My deep engrossment in the Bible story... had... an enduring effect.* **❞**

– SIGMUND FREUD

The result of religious ideas is that a person feels that a benevolent "Providence" is protecting them against the forces of nature. They are also reassured that death is not an extinction, but the beginning of a new existence. The moral laws that civilization is bound by are mirrored in laws that govern the universe. These universal laws are maintained by a supreme court of justice, so all good is rewarded and evil punished, if not in this life, then in the next. Depending on the religion, these attributes are bound up in one, or several, divine beings.

Having established the function of religion, Freud then looked at the real worth and place of religion. He found that religious ideas were not the result of experience or thinking, but illusions, "fulfilment of the oldest, strongest and most urgent wishes of mankind." He noted that illusions are not necessarily false – some are possible – but, "That the Messiah will come and found a golden age is much less likely." Whether one sees religious ideas as an illusion, or delusion, is up to the individual. He admitted that the assertions of religion cannot be refuted by reason, but considered that to be a lame excuse for accepting religion: "Ignorance is ignorance; no right to believe anything can be derived from it."

He argued that civilization ran a greater risk if the current attitude to religion continued than if it were given up. For Freud religion had achieved great things for civilization, but not enough, as it had ruled human society for thousands of years, but many people were still dissatisfied with society and unhappy living in it. The book quickly caused much controversy and attracted criticisms. In the 1935 revision to his autobiographical study Freud stated that his "essentially negative" view of religion had changed after *The Future of an Illusion*.

The summary of Freud's theories of culture, *Civilization and its Discontents* (see Chapter 15) included the characterization of religion as a "mass delusion … which succeeds in sparing many people an individual neurosis. But hardly anything more."

Freud often returned to the biblical stories of Joseph and Moses in his writings. He was fascinated with the figure of Moses for much of his adult life and had been obsessed with Michelangelo's statue of Moses from the time he saw it in the church of

BELOW *Vittore Carpaccio's painting of George slaying the dragon. Freud had a print of this in his collection. He would continue to be interested in myths and religion until his death.*

San Pietro in Vincoli on his first visit to Rome in 1901. Immediately after the Munich Congress of 1913, which saw the final split with Carl Jung (see Chapter 12), Freud spent three weeks studying the statue. This led to a paper called "The Moses of Michelangelo," published anonymously in *Imago* in 1914, though readers must have recognized his work. He carefully explores the placing of Moses' hands, and concludes that Moses had overcome his temptation to leap up and take vengeance, or cast down the (first) set of tablets. He then postulates that this is not the Moses of the Bible, but a different Moses, of Michelangelo's conception. Michelangelo had deviated from the biblical text in choosing to portray a superior Moses to the historical/traditional Moses, a Moses who is a "concrete expression of the highest mental achievement that is possible in man, that of struggling successfully against an inward

passion for the sake of a cause to which he had devoted himself."

Freud closely identified himself with Moses. He wrote to Jung in 1909, "If I am Moses then you are Joshua and will take possession of the promised land." He continued to be interested in Moses until the end of his life. Moses may have symbolized his own internal conflicts and his ambivalence about his Jewish roots. It has been suggested that writing *Moses and Monotheism* (see below) was an effort to resolve his uncertain identification with Moses, and his conflicted feelings toward his father.

Freud returned to his early intense exploration of biblical texts at the end of his life, with his last completed work, *Der Mann Moses und die monotheistische Religion* (*Moses and Monotheism*). He started work on *Moses and Monotheism* in Vienna in 1934; at that point he called it *The Man Moses, A Historical Novel*. This provocative book reflects his deep study of the Pentateuch and of critical scholarship, but is flawed by weak arguments and questionable methods. Freud himself acknowledged that he was not convinced of the historical aspects of the book.

His reason for researching and writing the book was that he was interested in the fact that the Jews were the first to sustain a permanently monotheistic religion. He wrote in a letter of 1937: "I started asking myself how the Jews acquired their particular character, and following my usual custom I went back to the earliest beginnings. I did not get far. I was astounded to find that already the first so-to-speak embryonic experience of the race, the influence of the man Moses and the exodus from Egypt, conditioned the entire further development up to the present day."

Freud's main controversial claim in the book was that Moses was not a Jew, but an Egyptian aristocrat, either a follower of Akhenaten, an ancient Egyptian monotheist, or Akhenaten himself. As he wrote, "To deprive a people of the man whom they take pride in as the greatest of their sons is not a thing to be gladly or carelessly undertaken." He also claimed that the monotheistic

religion that Moses gave to the Jews had Egyptian roots. In Freud's version of the story of Moses, Moses led his followers to freedom, but was prevented from entering the Holy Land because his followers rebelled against his insistence that they worship the Egyptian god Aten, and murdered him – a re-enactment of the murder of the father of a primal horde, which was the origin of religion in Freud's *Totem and Taboo*. Moses' followers took up a new religion based on the worship of the volcano god Yahweh. Some elements of Egyptian monotheism were preserved in the worship of Yahweh, such as circumcision. Finally, guilt from the murder of Moses was inherited through the generations, always driving the Jews to their religion. Freud claimed that the anti-Semitism directed at the Jews over the centuries was partly because of the Jews' refusal to acknowledge and atone for the murder of Moses.

He had not published any part of this book while still in Austria because he feared the outcome might be the banning of analysis in Vienna, owing to the strength of the Catholic Church in Austria, and its connection with politics. Colleagues questioned whether views expressed were any stronger than *The Future of an Illusion*, which had not been a cause for complaint.

Freud continued to work on the book while in exile in London. While there he received personal appeals and letters from several Jews imploring him not to publish it, as it might undermine their faith in their hour of need, but Freud felt they were overestimating any impact his work might have on believers. He described it as "an attack on religion only in so far as any scientific investigation of religious belief presupposes disbelief." In November he was interviewed by the committee of the Yiddish Scientific Institute and he spoke at length about the book and the warnings he had received not to publish it, concluding that to him, the truth was sacred and he could not renounce his rights as a scientist to voice it.

Freud managed to complete *Moses and Monotheism* before his operation in 1938 (see Chapter 19), and it was printed in German in Holland by August, his last completed book proving that he never resolved his ambivalence toward religion and all things religious.

Illness and Assisted Suicide

At Christmas 1938, Freud had to have a section of dead bone removed from his jaw, which gave him relief, but shortly after, a swelling appeared. There had been signs over the last two years that the cancer was returning, and early in February 1939, Max Schur was convinced that the swelling indicated a recurrence. Cancer expert Wilfred Trotter (1872–1939) examined Freud three times in February, but was not convinced it had recurred and recommended further observation. Schur was

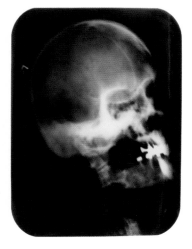

LEFT *Freud fleeing Austria in 1938. He wrote to his son Ernst that two prospects cheered him while waiting to leave Vienna: to see his family in London, and to die.*

ABOVE *An x-ray of Freud's jaw in February 1939 showing how much of his jaw and palate had been destroyed by cancer, or by the treatment.*

" *The goal of all life is death.* "

– SIGMUND FREUD

desperate to act, sure that the cancer had returned. He contacted Hans Pichler (see Chapter 13), who recommended electrocoagulation to kill the tissues, and radiation treatment. However, a Professor Lacassagne (1884–1971), brought from the Curie Institute in Paris, did not recommend the treatment. A biopsy confirmed a malignant recurrence, but it was now also considered inoperable, and from then on, the only treatment Freud received was palliative. He had daily treatments of Roentgen rays, which allowed him to continue to work a little longer, but he Freud suffered with increasing pain. In May, he wrote to Marie Bonaparte that "my world is again what it was before – a little island of pain floating on a sea of indifference."

He was keen to see *Moses and Monotheism* appear in English, writing to Arnold Zweig, "I am only waiting for Moses which is due to appear in March, and then I need not be interested in any book of mine again until my next reincarnation." Also in March the British Psycho-Analytical Society held a banquet in London to celebrate its 25th anniversary, but Freud was too ill to attend.

Visitors continued to come to Maresfield Gardens, and pupils and friends began to make last visits to see Freud, even while Martha and Anna became increasingly protective of him as his health worsened. There were no festivities for his 83rd birthday.

H. G. Wells was among those who often visited Freud in his last months. He had been trying to help him become naturalized since his arrival, and in 1939 was intending to gain British citizenship for Freud via an Act of Parliament. This idea greatly

Max Schur (1897–1969)

Freud and his personal doctor Deutsch parted ways after his cancer was initially diagnosed. In 1929, Marie Bonaparte convinced Freud that he needed a personal doctor to watch over his health and liaise with his surgeons. She suggested Max Schur, an internist who was analytically trained. Following his experience with Deutsch, Freud insisted on complete honesty from Schur in all instances. Schur and Freud would be very close for the last decade of Freud's life. Schur was torn when his quota number for the United States was called up in April 1939. He did not want to leave Freud, but he could not endanger the future of his family. He went to America, and took out his first naturalization papers, then returned to Freud in early July. He would be with him until the end, fulfilling his friend's last wishes.

pleased Freud, but he told Wells that perhaps there was no point because the Act would take longer to go through Parliament than Freud had left. Wells was unsuccessful and Freud had the status of "enemy alien" until his death.

Virginia (1882–1941) and Leonard (1880–1969) Woolf visited Freud in early 1939. Their press had been publishing the English editions of Freud's works since 1924, and from 1953, would bring out the *Standard Edition of the Complete Psychological Works of Sigmund Freud*, translated by the Stracheys (see Chapter 13). Virginia Woolf later recollected, "Nearly all famous men are disappointing or bores, or both. Freud was neither; he had an aura, not of fame, but of greatness."

Freud worked on two final papers that year, "An outline of Psychoanalysis," and "Some Elementary Lessons in Psychoanalysis," restating some of the basic points of psychoanalytic theory – perhaps to try and protect his legacy that little bit more – but he didn't finish either. Even at his age, and with

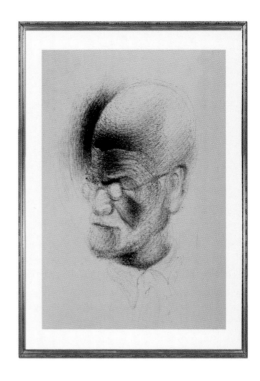

ABOVE *Freud by Salvador Dalí. Dalí completed several pictures of Freud after visiting him and sketching him in July 1938. Freud wasn't shown the sketch or finished drawing, as Stefan Zweig, who brought Dalí to see Freud, felt they conveyed Freud's imminent death.*

LEFT *Martha at the gate of 20 Maresfield Gardens in the 1940s. She lived there until she died, 12 years after her husband. Anna lived in the house until her own death in 1982.*

his pain and discomfort, he introduced some new concepts into these papers, such as the idea of the splitting of the ego in development. Freud thus demonstrated how creativity in science should always be based on fundamental principles, right until the end.

By the summer, he was much thinner and was having trouble sleeping. The cancer spread through his cheek. He did not like taking drugs, preferring to keep his mind clear to work, and instead using hot-water bottles to ease his pain, but he was now prepared to take aspirin as well. Even at this stage he rarely complained of his pain to friends or visitors. Freud is often characterized as being stoic in the face of his cancer, but this was not simply a passive acceptance of his fate. It has been suggested that he formed an active relationship with his cancer, taking an analytic attitude to the illness. His illness also entered his work, and in some of his later works, such as *Civilization and its Discontents*, it is clear that he was thinking of his cancer, and the methods and technology used to combat it, as he wrote.

ABOVE *Freud loved flowers and gardens, and the garden at Maresfield Gardens gave him much pleasure. He could see the gardens from the sickbed in his study where he spent his last days, and where he died.*

LEFT *Freud's funerary urn at Golders Green Crematorium, a gift given to him by Marie Bonaparte for his 75th birthday. When Martha died, 12 years later, her ashes were added to the urn.*

BELOW *On August 1, 1939, Freud closed his practice. That day, he was visited by Hanns* *Sachs, Marie Bonaparte, and her husband, Prince George of Greece.*

Freud continued to work for four hours a day until just seven weeks before he died, when he finally closed his practice on August 1, 1939, after 57 years of treating patients. He was now very weak and ill and hardly ate. He spent his time in a sick bay in his study, where he could watch the garden. He read the newspapers, following the events leading up to the outbreak of the war, and the opening moves of Hitler's armies.

By mid-September he was sleeping most of the time, but on September 21 he was able to remind Schur of the promise he had extracted from the doctor the first time they met: "You promised me then you would help me when I could no longer carry on. It is only torture now and it has no longer any sense." Schur agreed, and Freud thanked him, asking him to tell Anna of the talk. Anna wanted to postpone the inevitable, but Schur persuaded her that it was time. The following day, Schur gave Freud the first of several doses of morphine. He fell into a peaceful sleep, and after the second dose, he lapsed into a coma. He died in his study just before midnight on September 23, 1939.

Freud was cremated three days later, and his ashes lie at Golders Green Crematorium in one of a favorite pair of Greek urns from his collection. Speeches were given by Stefan Zweig and Ernest Jones.

TELEPHONE: HAMPSTEAD 0344.
TELEGRAMS:
ACIDNESS, SWISS, LONDON.

N⁰ 375843

THE PRESCRIPTION

Prof. S. Freud
20, Mansfield Gdns

DISPENSED BY

T. H. BATEMAN & CO. Lᵀᴰ

B. JONES, M.P.S.
H. C. HEARD, M.P.S.

DISPENSING CHEMISTS,

223, FINCHLEY ROAD, N.W.3

Bateman chemists dispensed medication for Freud while
he was living at Maresfield Gardens. This 1939 prescription
was strychnine for his heart.

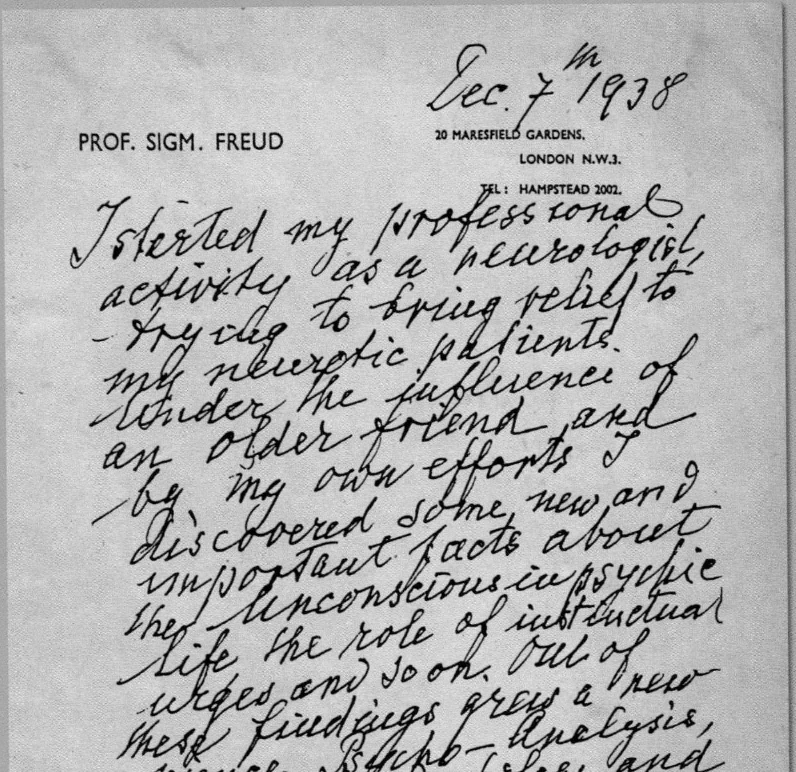

PROF. SIGM. FREUD

20 MARESFIELD GARDENS,
LONDON N.W.3.
TEL: HAMPSTEAD 2002.

Dec. 7th 1938

I started my professional activity as a neurologist, trying to bring relief to my neurotic patients. Under the influence of an older friend and by my own efforts I discovered some new and important facts about the unconscious in psychic life the role of instinctual urges and so on. Out of these findings grew a new science, Psycho-Analysis, a part of Psychology and a new method of treatment of the neuroses. I had to pay heavily for this bit of good luck. People did not believe in my facts and thought my theories unsavoury. Resistance was strong and unrelenting. In—

On December 7, 1938, Freud recorded a short statement he had written in English for the BBC summarizing his scientific career. The recording of his voice betrays his obvious effort to clearly enunciate the words for the microphone, battling with his illness all the way. This summary is rather modest given the huge body of work he had created over six decades.

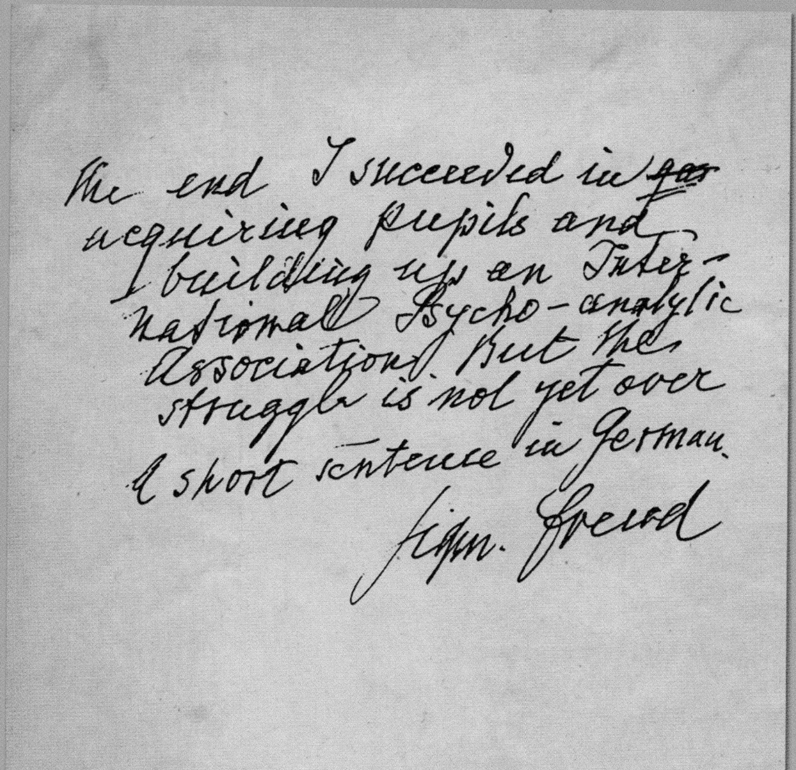

the end I succeeded in the
acquiring pupils and
building up an Inter-
national Psycho-analytic
Association. But the
struggle is not yet over

A short sentence in German.

Sigm. Freud

Freud's Legacy

Some have said that Freud left two important legacies: his psychoanalytic theories, and his daughter Anna, the only one of his children to follow him into the realm of psychoanalysis. She taught at a school before becoming her father's pupil, began practicing as an analyst in 1922, and by 1925 was the chairman of the Vienna Society. Her first major contribution to psychoanalytic theory was her first book, *The Ego and the Mechanisms of Defence*, published in 1937, which built upon Freud's ideas. She presented it to him on his 80th birthday.

Anna was a pioneer of child analysis. She adapted psychoanalytic techniques to be suitable for children, using play and games, and sometimes art. This kind of therapy lets children demonstrate fears, defences, and fantasies through play, allowing the analysts to observe carefully, watching for recurring themes. Melanie Klein, based first in Berlin, then in London, also developed a play technique for use with children, but differences between the two leaders in child analysis and their ideas were never resolved, despite exchange visits between Vienna and London. Later, they disagreed over the treatment of adults, resulting in the creation of two separate training groups.

Anna applied her findings to education, and opened an experimental kindergarten for children from poorer areas of Vienna in 1937 with Dorothy Burlingham. After emigrating to England, she spent the war running a residential children's community in London for orphans and children separated from their parents, with a branch for older children in the country. During the war she published several books with Dorothy Burlingham: *Young Children in Wartime*, *Infants Without Families*, and *War and Children*. After her father's and then mother's death, Anna remained at 20 Maresfield Gardens, with Dorothy.

LEFT *Anna Freud c.1970. She devoted her life to psychoanalysis, and it was her wish that the family home would become a museum to honor her father after her death. The museum now celebrates the life and work of Sigmund and Anna Freud.*

BELOW *Clement Freud when an MP, though many knew him best as a panellist on the BBC Radio 4 show,* Just a Minute, *which he participated in from 1967 until his death in 2009.*

After the war, a course in child analysis was instituted, followed by Anna's founding of the Hampstead Child Therapy Clinic, of which she was director from 1952 until her death in 1982. The facilities were of great help to Anna, and her work there was integral to her most important book *Normality and Pathology in Childhood* (1965). She would defend her father's basic theories until her death, even though she did not follow his every idea.

Only one other of Freud's descendants is known to have taken up psychoanalysis: daughter Sophie's surviving son, Ernst, who practiced under the name Ernst W. Freud in Germany and Great Britain. While the other Freud children did not follow their father's calling, they have proved anything but an average family, achieving success in such varied fields as academia, writing, fashion, social work, finance, media, politics, and entertainment. Most of the Freud family emigrated to Britain during the war, and the family has been described as "a dynasty that dominates the London social scene." Freud's youngest son Ernst emigrated to London after the Nazis came to power, where he continued to be a successful architect. His three sons all forged their own paths. Possibly the best known of the three was Lucian Freud (1922–2011), considered the pre-eminent British artist of his time. From the 1950s, he painted almost exclusively portraits, often nudes, and friends, family, and other artists. His paintings are noted for their psychological depth,

> **❝** *A good noble human being is an unfailing source of joy, sympathy, and admiration.* **❞**
>
> – SIGMUND FREUD

aiming to capture the individuality of the sitter. Lucian Freud's children include fashion designer Bella Freud (1961–) writer Esther Freud (1963–), and artist Jane McAdam Freud (1958–).

Ernst's youngest son, Sir Clement Freud (1924–2009) – his name Anglicized from Clemens – had a varied career. During the Second World War he was aide to Field Marshal Montgomery and worked at the Nuremberg Trials. He then became one of Britain's first celebrity chefs, and was an award-winning food and drink writer, writing various newspaper and magazine columns and two children's books. He became a household name after appearing in dog food commercials on television. In 1973, he became Liberal Member of Parliament for the Isle of Ely. Upon leaving Parliament in 1987, he was granted a knighthood. Clement claimed to have never read a word of his grandfather's writings, and his grandson Jack commented, "I'm pretty useless at psychology … I feel a bit guilty at letting the family name down, but I'm sure that there are quite enough Freudian psychologists to go round."

On the other side of the Atlantic, Edward L. Bernays (1891–1995), Freud's nephew, was a pioneer in the field of public relations, combining Freud's psychoanalytical ideas with theories of crowd psychology to try to manipulate public opinion. His work helped to popularize Freud's theories in the United States. He published the first book on public relations in 1923, and would go on to write extensively about democracy and the role of public relations within a democratic society. He was listed as one of the 100 most influential Americans of the twentieth century by *Time* magazine. George Loewenstein (1955–), grandson of Martin Freud, is a professor at Carnegie Mellon University, in Economics and Psychology.

Since Sigmund Freud's death, psychoanalysis has spread widely throughout the Western world, particularly in the United States in the post-war years. The IPA accredits psychoanalytic training centres throughout the world, including six in the United States.

It would not surprise Freud himself that he has been the focus of much harsh criticism since his death. He is often accused of not having evidence, and not being a real scientist: "Freud was already a pseudo-scientist from the hour he published *The Interpretation of Dreams*" (Frederick Crews, 1988). Those who have read Freud's writings are rarely ambivalent, feeling either admiration, or blind hatred for him. His theories are often misunderstood, or misrepresented.

Inevitably, psychoanalysis has been further developed since Freud's time. Aspects of his thinking, such as some of his ideas on female sexuality, have been developed or abandoned by psychoanalysts. The main psychoanalytic theories can be grouped in several theoretical schools, with the traditional British and American psychoanalysis being "ego psychology", while Lacanian psychoanalysis has had a major influence on psychoanalysis in France and parts of Latin America. Variations in therapeutic technique have also developed, and while sessions for one

ABOVE Silver medals minted in the Czech Republic and designed by Freud's great-grandaughter, Jane McAdam Freud, for the 70th anniversary of his death.

RIGHT A statue of Freud, sculpted by Oscar Nemon, stands in front of the Tavistock Institute, on the corner of Belsize Lane and Fitzjohns Avenue, London.

OPPOSITE An early painting by Lucian Freud, which he gave to his aunt Anna.

FREUD

patient remain the norm, psychoanalytic therapy is also used in group situations. Child analysis was developed by Anna Freud during Freud's lifetime.

The least popular parts of Freud's theories are probably the Oedipus complex, with associated ideas of castration anxiety and penis envy (see Chapter 10). There is also a continuing debate about the unconscious (see Chapter 9), including how much goes on in the unconscious and how it affects our behavior. Some theorists do not use the concept of the unconscious at all. It can be argued, however, that awareness of the unconscious and how it might be affecting someone makes it possible to communicate with those suffering from even the most severe mental illnesses. Also, even if the idea of an unconscious does not fit comfortably, it is clear that we all manipulate reality, and our memories of reality, to suit our needs, so Freud's theories of defences of the ego can help us understand how and why we do this.

Regardless of the revisions and changes in psychoanalysis, it is impossible for anyone involved in psychology, psychiatry, neurology, or related fields to avoid Freud. While traditional Freudian psychoanalysis is not commonly practiced, aspects of his thinking are woven into most approaches.

Freud himself abandoned his early seduction theory, but his interest in trauma in childhood, and how the events of childhood affect a person in later life, has had far-reaching implications, leading to child psychology, and the recognition of the importance of protecting children from trauma and abuse as they grow up. Historically, children were seen and treated as small adults, but his work on psychosexual stages of development, while now rarely used, means that it is now normal to think about stages of development during childhood.

Freud's therapeutic model of the talking cure and free association (see Chapter 7) continue to be important. While therapies have evolved significantly, no one would deny that talking helps, and most therapy includes talking in a relaxed atmosphere. While transference is contested, the nature of the therapeutic relationship in general is accepted as important to success, just as Freud considered it to be. Outside professional therapy, the publication and spread of his ideas mean that people can also choose to examine the events of their own past themselves using free association, or by talking with others in a way that would not have been appropriate, or acceptable, before Freud. It has been suggested that Freud's work has "opened up" society so people can now talk to each other much more honestly.

While Freud's emphasis on sexuality was always an unpopular part of psychoanalytic theory, he did manage to bring sexuality out into the open. This achievement is not to be underestimated in the context of the late nineteenth century, when the topic was avoided, particularly by women and the middle and upper classes.

Outside of the therapeutic and clinical uses of psychoanalysis, Freud's ideas have influenced the humanities. There have been psychoanalytic

discussions of figures in art, literature and so on, from Freud's earliest followers onwards. It has been said that the psychoanalytic tradition is possibly more original and creative than any other intellectual tradition of the twentieth century, and those who have come after Freud have cast their net widely in terms of subject matter. However, psychoanalytic theory is also often superficially applied in literary and film criticism, other branches of the humanities, and also politics.

Freud was a pioneer, and one of the twentieth century's greatest thinkers, writing for over 50 years about a huge range of subject matter. Even though most people will never read or fully understand his extensive writings, he revolutionized how people think about the mind, and in a society where we pepper our conversation with talk of "anxiety," "repression," "ego," and "guilt," it is clear that his ideas are part of our everyday language and culture.

ABOVE LEFT *Karen Horney (1885–1952), German psychoanalyst. Horney questioned some of Freud's theories, particularly that of sexuality, and she is often classified as "neo-Freudian." Neo-Freudians were psychiatrists and psychologists of the mid-20th century, who were all influenced by Freud, but extended his theories, often in cultural or social directions. Adler was the first to explore these areas, and it has also been suggested that Horney be more properly described as "neo-Adlerian."*

ABOVE RIGHT *Jacques Lacan (1901–1981), French psychoanalyst and psychiatrist. A self-professed Freudian, he has been called the "most controversial psychoanalyst since Freud." His regular seminars, run for nearly 30 years, and his "return to Freud" have had a significant impact on many disciplines.*

Translations

Sources

Page 62: Letter to Wilhelm Fleiss
Freud begins his letter to Fleiss by recounting a recent incident when he met Fleiss' wife and son. He remarks that though Fleiss' son was in good spirits, his wife was clearly worried about her mother's ill-health. Freud also touches on his relationship with Josef Breuer and how greatly it pains him that their relationship had been broken beyond repair. Eventually, however, he announces that he no longer wants to dwell on that and instead talks to Fleiss about his work, including the essay about dreams, which he is doing without much pleasure. Freud also tells his friend it pains him that he is collating material for a book he refers to as *The Psychology of Everyday Life* (this would eventually become *The Psychopathology of Everyday Life*). At the end of the letter, Freud makes his first mention of the "Dora" case to Fleiss, remarking that he is excited to have a new patient who has been responding well to his treatments. Freud completes his letter by informing Fleiss that there was a review of *The Interpretation of Dreams* in the *Muncher allegemaine Zeitung* (*Munich General Newspaper*) on October 12, 1900, which he dismissed as foolish. In fact, the review was not actually critical, but for the most part simply consisted of quotes from the book.

Page 125: "A Word on Anti-Semitism"
In this essay Freud provides a summary of another piece of writing defending the Jewish people. Writing from a Christian perspective, the unknown author claims that, as a religion of love that is based on the knowledge that Jesus sacrificed his life to offer a salvation from sin, it went against the principles of Christianity to allow Jews to be mistreated. The writer went on to say that Jewish people had been treated unfairly for centuries and that this attitude was continuing, despite the fact that Jews could not be considered inferior. Freud's biographer, Ernest Jones, believed that the unknown author Freud was summarizing, was actually none other than Freud himself.

Page 131: Freud's Personal Diary
The first page covers April–August 1933, which was the period in which the Nazi's burnt copies of Freud's books. The second page describes September 1937–March 1938. Notable events include the speech Kurt Schuschnigg gave to the Australian Federal Diet in which he stated that "Austria would go thus far and no further," Schuschnigg's resignation on March 11, Anschluss with Austria on March 13, Hitler's entry into Vienna on March 14 and on March 15 Freud noted that his home and the Verlag had been visited by Nazis. The entries for March 16 and 17 are intriguing – respectively they read "Jones" and "Princess." The former refers to Ernest Jones and the latter to Princes Marie Bonaparte, both of whom were trying to keep Freud and his family safe. The final entry on this page, dated March 22, simply notes that Anna was now in the hands of the Gestapo.

Page 11: *"a new and deeper science of the mind which would be ... indispensable for the understanding of the normal."*
Sigmund Freud, "An Autobiographical Study" (1924), in Peter Gay (ed.) *The Freud Reader* (Vintage Books, London, 1995), p. 30.

Page 14: *"what [was] neurotic, but also what [was] intense."*
Letter from Freud to Wilhelm Fliess, October 3, 1897, as appears in in Peter Gay (ed.) *The Freud Reader* (Vintage Books, London, 1995), p. 113.

Page 18: *"strange scholarly society"*
Letter from Freud to Martha Bernays, February 7, 1884, in Ernst L. Freud (ed.), *Letters of Sigmund Freud* (Dover, Mineaola, NY, 1992), letter 37.

Page 19: *"godless Jew"*
Letter from Freud to Oskar Pfister, October 9, 1918, in S. Freud, O. Pfister (Ernst Freud, Heinrich Meng, eds.) *Psychoanalysis and Faith: The Letters of Sigmund Freud and Oskar Pfister* (trans. E. Mosbacher) (Chatto & Windus, 1963), p. 64.

Page 31: *"classical hysterical hemianaesthesia"*
Sigmund Freud, "An Autobiographical Study" (1924), in Peter Gay (ed.) *The Freud Reader* (Vintage Books, London, 1995), p. 8.

Page 32: *"normal euphoria"*
Freud, Uber Coca (1885), in Ernest Jones, *The Life and Work of Sigmund Freud* (edited and abridged by Lionel Trilling and Steven Marcus) (Basic Books, New York, 1961), p. 56.

Page 37: *"the third scourge of humanity"*
Albrecht Erlenmayer, 1885, quoted in Frank J. Sulloway, *Freud, Biologist of the Mind: Beyond the Psychoanalytic Legend* (Harvard University Press, MA, 1992), p. 26.

Page 38: *"In the autumn of 1886 I settled down in Vienna as a physician, and married the girl who had been waiting for me in a distant city for more than four years."*
Sigmund Freud, "An Autobiographical Study" (1924), in Peter Gay (ed.) *The Freud Reader* (Vintage Books, London, 1995), p. 7.

Page 50: *"a talking cure"*
Sigmund Freud and Joseph Breuer, Case Histories, Case I Fraulein Anna O. (1895), in Peter Gay (ed.) *The Freud Reader* (Vintage Books, London, 1995), p. 68.

Page 55: *"expression of a fragmentary activity of the brain, as the authorities have claimed"*
Sigmund Freud, "The Interpretation of Dreams" (1900), in Peter Gay (ed.) *The Freud Reader* (Vintage Books, London, 1995), p. 142.

Page 57: *"latent dream-thoughts"*
Sigmund Freud, "On Dreams" (1911), in Peter Gay (ed.) *The Freud Reader* (Vintage Books, London, 1995), p. 148.

Page 61: *"royal road to the unconscious"*
Sigmund Freud, *The Interpretation of Dreams* (2nd ed., 1909) ch. 7, sect. E.

Page 61: *"Insight such as this falls to one's lot but once in a lifetime."*
Sigmund Freud, preface to third English edition of *The Interpretation of Dreams*, in Ernest Jones, *The Life and Work of Sigmund Freud* (edited and abridged by Lionel Trilling and Steven Marcus) (Basic Books, New York, 1961), p. 228.

Page 72: *"I was able to show from a short story ... called Gradiva ..., that invented dreams can be interpreted in the same way as real ones and that the unconscious mechanisms familiar to us in the 'dream-work' are thus also operative in the processes of imaginative writing."*

Sigmund Freud, "An Autobiographical Study" (1924), in Peter Gay (ed.) *The Freud Reader* (Vintage Books, London, 1995), p. 40.

Page 76: *"splendid isolation"*
Sigmund Freud (trans. A. A. Brill), "The History of the Psychoanalytic Movement," *Nervous and Mental Disease Monograph Series* (1917, no.25), I.

Pages 78–79: *"The neurotic symptoms must have been one of the ways in which the unconscious material was indirectly trying to emerge, and without this pressure it is doubtful whether Freud would have made the progress he did."*
Ernest Jones, *The Life and Work of Sigmund Freud* (edited and abridged by Lionel Trilling and Steven Marcus) (Basic Books, New York, 1961), p.198.

Page 79: *"The death of the old man has affected me profoundly. I valued him highly, understood him very well, and ... he meant a great deal to me."*
Letter from Freud to Wilhelm Fliess, 2 November 1896 in Ernst L. Freud (ed.), Letters of Sigmund Freud (Dover, Mineaola, NY, 1992), letter 152.

Page 79: *"most important event, the most poignant loss, of a man's life"*
Sigmund Freud, preface to second edition of *The Interpretation of Dreams* (1908), in Ernest Jones, *The Life and Work of Sigmund Freud* (edited and abridged by Lionel Trilling and Steven Marcus) (Basic Books, New York, 1961), p. 213.

Page 79: *"high point of my life"*
Letter from Freud to Wilhelm Fliess, September 19, 1901, in Ernst Freud, Lucie Freud and Ilse Grubrich-Simitis (ed.) *Sigmund Freud: His life in pictures and words* (W. W. Norton & Co., New York, 1985), p. 168.

Page 79 *"My recovery can only come about through work in the unconscious. I cannot manage with conscious efforts alone."*
Letter from Freud to Wilhelm Fliess, late April 1897, in Ernest Jones, *The Life and Work of Sigmund Freud* (edited and abridged by Lionel Trilling and Steven Marcus) (Basic Books, New York, 1961), p. 213.

Page 79–80: *"My self-analysis is in fact the most essential thing I have at present and it promises to become of the greatest value to me if it reaches its end."*
Letter from Freud to Wilhelm Fliess, October 15, 1897, in Ernst Freud, Lucie Freud and Ilse Grubrich-Simitis (ed.) *Sigmund Freud: His life in pictures and words* (W. W. Norton & Co., New York, 1985), p. 156.

Page 81: *"at an hour when most old ladies would be in bed"*
Ernest Jones, *The Life and Work of Sigmund Freud* (edited and abridged by Lionel Trilling and Steven Marcus) (Basic Books, New York, 1961), p. 4.

Page 81: *"I have found, in my own case too, being in love with my mother and jealous of my father, and I now consider it a universal event in early childhood."*
Letter from Freud to Wilhelm Fliess, October 15, 1897, in Peter Gay (ed.) *The Freud Reader* (Vintage Books, London, 1995), p. 116.

Page 82: *"My style in it was bad, because I was feeling too well physically; I have to be somewhat miserable in order to write well."*
Letter from Freud to Wilhelm Fliess, September 6, 1899, in Ernest Jones, *The Life and Work of Sigmund Freud* (edited and abridged by Lionel Trilling and Steven Marcus) (Basic Books, New York, 1961), p. 213.

Page 85: *"son and heir"*
Ernest Jones, *The Life and Work of Sigmund Freud* (edited and abridged by Lionel Trilling and Steven Marcus) (Basic Books, New York, 1961), p.253.

Page 87: *"developing backwards"*
Freud, as quoted in Ernest Jones, *The Life and Work of Sigmund Freud* (edited and abridged by Lionel Trilling and Steven Marcus) (Basic Books, New York, 1961), p. 313.

Page 88: *"go into unsavoury details"*
Ernest Jones, *The Life and Work of Sigmund Freud* (edited and abridged by Lionel Trilling and Steven Marcus) (Basic Books, New York, 1961), p.318.

Page 89: *"as an acid does a salt"*
Letter from Freud to Sándor Ferenczi, May 13, 1913, E. Brabant, E Falzedar, Patrizia Giampieri-Deutsch (eds.), *The Correspondence of Sigmund Freud and Sándor Ferenczi, 1908–1914* (Harvard University Press, 1993), No. 395.

Page 90: *"watered down"*
Sigmund Freud, "An Autobiographical Study" (1924), in Peter Gay (ed.), *The Freud Reader* (Vintage Books, London, 1995), p. 33.

Page 90–91: *"I know that I am writing for only five people in the present, you and the few others [Abraham, Rank, Sachs and Jones]."*
Freud to Sandor Ferenczi, late 1914, quoted in Ernest Jones, *The Life and Work of Sigmund Freud* (edited and abridged by Lionel Trilling and Steven Marcus) (Basic Books, New York, 1961), p. 339.

Page 91: *"bitter end"*
Letter from Freud to Sándor Ferenczi October 9, 1917, Freud–Ferenczi correspondence, Freud Collection LC, as quoted in Peter Gay, *Freud: A Life for our Time* (W. W. Norton, 1999), p. 372. Jones, Ernest Jones, *The Life and Work of Sigmund Freud* (edited and abridged by Lionel Trilling and Steven Marcus) (Basic Books, New York, 1961), p. 350.

Page 97: *"starving and impoverished subjects of the Central European states"*
Sigmund Freud, "An Autobiographical Study" (1924), in Peter Gay (ed.), *The Freud Reader* (Vintage Books, London, 1995), p. 34.

Page 98: *"My little Sophie ... broke the surprising news that she is engaged to you. We realize that this fact makes us, so to speak, superfluous and that there is nothing left for us to do but go through the formality of bestowing our blessing."*
Letter from Freud to Max Halberstadt, July 7, 1912, in Ernst L Freud (ed.), Letters of Sigmund Freud (Dover, Mineaola, NY, 1992), letter 152.

Page 98: *"The loss of a child seems to be a serious, narcissistic injury; what is known as mourning will probably follow only later."*
Letter from Freud to Oscar Pfister, January 27, 1920, in Ernst L Freud (ed.), Letters of Sigmund Freud (Dover, Mineaola, NY, 1992), letter 186.

Page 100: *"He was very weak, never entirely free of a temperature, one of those children whose mental development grows at the expense of its physical strength."*
Letter from Freud to Katá and Lajos Levy, June 11, 1923, in Ernst L Freud (ed.), Letters of Sigmund Freud (Dover, Mineaola, NY, 1992), letter 203.

Page 101: *"the monster"*
Ernest Jones, *The Life and Work of Sigmund Freud* (edited and abridged by Lionel Trilling and Steven Marcus) (Basic Books, New York, 1961), p. 443.

Page 102: *"for the natural end"*
Ernest Jones, *The Life and Work of Sigmund Freud* (edited and abridged by Lionel Trilling and Steven Marcus) (Basic Books, New York, 1961), p. 447.

Page 106: *"We shall now look upon the individual as a psychical id, unknown and unconscious, upon whose surface rests the ego."*
Sigmund Freud, *The Ego and the Id* (1923), in Peter Gay (ed.), *The Freud Reader* (Vintage Books, London, 1995), p. 635.

Page 106–7: *"The ego represents what may be called reason and common sense, in contrast to the id, which contains the passions."*
Sigmund Freud, *The Ego and the Id* (1923), in Peter Gay (ed.), *The Freud Reader* (Vintage Books, London, 1995), p. 636.

Page 107: *"contains the germ from which all religions have evolved"*
Sigmund Freud, *The Ego and the Id* (1923), in Peter Gay (ed.), *The Freud Reader* (Vintage Books, London, 1995), p. 643.

Page 107: "*smoking is one of the greatest and cheapest enjoyments in life*"
Peter Gay, *Freud: A Life for our Time* (W. W. Norton, 1999), p. 170.

Page 118: "*residues of the existences of countless egos*"
Sigmund Freud, *The Ego and the Id* (1923), in Peter Gay (ed.), *The Freud Reader* (Vintage Books, London, 1995), p. 644.

Page 108: "*a poor creature owing service to three masters and consequently menaced by three dangers: from the external world, from the libido of the id and from the severity of the super-ego.*"
Sigmund Freud, *The Ego and the Id* (1923), in Peter Gay (ed.), *The Freud Reader* (Vintage Books, London, 1995), p. 656.

Page 108: "*Psycho-analysis is an instrument to enable the ego to achieve a progressive conquest of the id.*"
Sigmund Freud, *The Ego and the Id* (1923), in Peter Gay (ed.), *The Freud Reader* (Vintage Books, London, 1995), p. 656.

Page 112: "*uncharted terrain*"
Peter Gay (ed.), *The Freud Reader* (Vintage Books, London, 1995), p. 594.

Page 116: "*doomed to decay and dissolution and which cannot even do without pain and anxiety as warning signals*"
Sigmund Freud, *Civilization and its Discontents*, in Peter Gay (ed.), *The Freud Reader* (Vintage Books, London, 1995), p. 729.

Page 117: "*It deals with civilization, consciousness of guilt, happiness and similar lofty matters.*"
Letter from Freud to Lou Andreas-Salomé, July 28, 1929, in Ernst L Freud (ed.), *Letters of Sigmund Freud* (Dover, Mineaola, NY, 1992), letter 243.

Page 118: "*No pain, no grief, which is probably to be explained by the circumstances, the great age and the end of the pity we had felt at her helplessness. With that a feeling of liberation ... I was not allowed to die as long as she was alive, and now I may.*"
Letter from Freud to Sándor Ferenczi, September 16, 1930, in Ernst L Freud (ed.), *Letters of Sigmund Freud* (Dover, Mineaola, NY, 1992), letter 256.

Page 118: "*I am too old, and working with me is too precarious. I should not need to work any longer.*"
Freud, 1932, Ernest Jones, *The Life and Work of Sigmund Freud* (edited and abridged by Lionel Trilling and Steven Marcus), (Basic Books, New York, 1961), p. 489.

Page 119: "*What progress we are making. In the Middle Ages they would have burnt me; nowadays they are content with burning my books.*"
Ernest Jones, *The Life and Work of Sigmund Freud* (edited and abridged by Lionel Trilling and Steven Marcus), (Basic Books, New York, 1961), p. 496.

Page 120: "*no likelihood of our being able to suppress humanity's aggressive tendencies*"
Letter from Freud to Einstein, September 1932, published as Warum krieg (1932) and quoted in Otto Nathan and Heinz Norden (ed.), *Einstein on Peace* (New York: Schocken Books, 1960), pp.186–203.

Page 121: "*Our loss is great and painful ... Ferenczi takes with him a part of the old time; then with my departure another will begin...*"
Letter from Freud to Ernest Jones, May 29, 1933, *The Complete Correspondence of Sigmund Freud and Ernest Jones 1908–1939* (edited by R Andrew Paskauskas and with an introduction by Riccardi Steiner), (Harvard University Press, Cambridge, Massachusetts, 1995), p. 721.

Page 121: "*although I have been exceptionally happy in my home, with my wife and children ... I nevertheless cannot reconcile myself to the wretchedness and helplessness of old age, and look forward with a kind of longing to the transition into non-existence.*"
Letter from Freud to Stefan Zweig, May 18, 1936, in Ernst L Freud (ed.), *Letters of Sigmund Freud* (Dover, Mineaola, NY, 1992), letter 284.

Page 121: "*... tortured as I am by the conflict between the desire for rest, the dread of renewed suffering ..., and by the anticipation of sorrow at being separated from everything to which I am still attached*"
Letter from Freud to Marie Bonaparte, December 6, 1936 in Ernst L Freud (ed.), *Letters of Sigmund Freud* (Dover, Mineaola, NY, 1992), letter 288.

Page 121: "*our little bit of civil war was not at all nice*"
Letter from Freud to Arnold Zweig, February 25, 1934, in Ernst Freud, Lucie Freud and Ilse Grubrich-Simitis (ed.), *Sigmund Freud: His life in pictures and words* (W. W. Norton & Co., New York: 1985), p. 263.

Page 122: "*for us old people*"
Letter from Freud to Ernest Jones, May 13, 1938, in Ernst Freud, Lucie Freud and Ilse Grubrich-Simitis (ed.), *Sigmund Freud: His life in pictures and words* (W. W. Norton & Co., New York: 1985), p. 263.

Page 123: "*Everything is in a certain sense unreal, we are no longer here and not yet there.*"
Letter from Freud to Minna Bernays, May 26, 1938, quoted in Peter Gay, "Sigmund and Minna? The Biographer as Voyeur," *New York Times* (January 29, 1989).

Page 128: "*In short, for the first time and late in life I have experienced what it is to be famous.*"
Letter from Freud to Alexander Freud, June 22, 1938, in Ernst L Freud (ed.), *Letters of Sigmund Freud* (Dover, Mineaola, NY, 1992), letter 301.

Page 128: "*rather strange, difficult and often bewildering*"
Letter from Freud to Marie Bonaparte, October 4, 1938, in Ernst L Freud (ed.), *Letters of Sigmund Freud* (Dover, Mineaola, NY, 1992), letter 305.

Page 129: "*I can hardly write, no better than I can speak or smoke.*"
Letter from Freud to Marie Bonaparte, October 4, 1938, in Ernst Freud (ed.), *Letters of Sigmund Freud* (Dover, Mineaola, NY, 1992), letter 305.

Page 132: "*My parents were Jews and I have remained a Jew myself*"
Sigmund Freud, "An Autobiographical Study" (1924), in Peter Gay (ed.), *The Freud Reader* (Vintage Books, London, 1995), p. 3.

Page 132: "*My language is German. My culture, my attainments are German. I considered myself German intellectually, until I noticed the growth of anti-Semitic prejudice in Germany and German Austria. Since that time, I prefer to call myself a Jew.*"
Freud, quoted in George Sylvester Viereck, *Glimpses of the Great* (Duckworth, London, 1930), p. 34.

Page 132: "*Neither in my private life nor in my writings have I ever made a secret of my being an out-and-out unbeliever*"
Freud to a correspondent, 1938, in Peter Gay (ed.), *The Freud Reader* (Vintage Books, London, 1995), p. xix.

Page 134: "*give expression to their piety*"
Sigmund Freud, Obsessive actions and religious practices (1907), in Peter Gay (ed.), *The Freud Reader* (Vintage Books, London, 1995), p. 429.

Page 134: "*perhaps the most important item in the psychical inventory of a civilization.*"
Sigmund Freud, Future of an illusion, 1927, in Peter Gay (ed.), *The Freud Reader* (Vintage Books, London, 1995), p. 692.

Page 136: "*fulfilment of the oldest, strongest and most urgent wishes of mankind*".
Sigmund Freud, Future of an illusion, 1927, VI, in Peter Gay (ed.), *The Freud Reader* (Vintage Books, London, 1995), p. 703.

Page 136: "*That the Messiah will come and found a golden age is much less likely.*"
Sigmund Freud, Future of an illusion, 1927, VI, in Peter Gay (ed.),
The Freud Reader (Vintage Books, London, 1995), p. 704.

Page 136-7: "*Ignorance is ignorance; no right to believe anything can be derived from it.*"
Sigmund Freud, Future of an illusion, 1927, VI, in Peter Gay (ed.), *The Freud Reader* (Vintage Books, London, 1995), p. 705.

Page 137: "*mass delusion ... which succeeds in sparing many people an individual neurosis. But hardly anything more*"
Sigmund Freud, Civilization and its discontents, II, in Peter Gay (ed.), *The Freud Reader* (Vintage Books, London, 1995), p. 735.

Page 138: "*concrete expression of the highest mental achievement that is possible in man, that of struggling successfully against an inward passion for the sake of a cause to which he had devoted himself*"
Freud, Moses and Monotheism (1939), in *Complete Psychological Works of Sigmund Freud, Vol. 23*, (trans. James Strachey), (Vintage Classics, London, 2001), p. 7.

Page 138: "*If I am Moses then you are Joshua and will take possession of the promised land.*"
Letter from Freud to Carl Jung, 1909, in *The Freud–Jung Letters* (Mcguire, William, ed.) Trans. by Ralph Mannheim and R F C Hull), (Bollingen Series XCIV, Princeton University Press, Princeton, 1974) p. 196.

Page 138: "*I started asking myself how the Jews acquired their particular character, and following my usual custom I went back to the earliest beginnings. I did not get far. I was astounded to find that already the first so-to-speak embryonic experience of the race, the influence of the man Moses and the exodus from Egypt, conditioned the entire further development up to the present day.*"
Letter from Freud to anon., December 14, 1937, in Ernst Freud, Lucie Freud and Ilse Grubrich-Simitis (ed.) *Sigmund Freud: His life in pictures and words* (W. W. Norton & Co., New York: 1985), p. 319.

Page 138-39: "*To deprive a people of the man whom they take pride in as the greatest of their sons is not a thing to be gladly or carelessly undertaken.*"
Freud, Moses and Monotheism (1939), in *Complete Psychological Works of Sigmund Freud, Vol. 23*, (trans. James Strachey), (Vintage Classics, London, 2001), p. 7.

Page 139: "*an attack on religion only in so far as any scientific investigation of religious belief presupposes disbelief*"
Letter from Sigmund Freud to Charles Singer, October 31, 1938 in in Ernst L Freud (ed.), *Letters of Sigmund Freud* (Dover, Mineaola, NY, 1992), letter 307.

Page 141: "*my world is again what it was before – a little island of pain floating on a sea of indifference*"
Letter from Freud to Marie Bonaparte, May 1939, in Ernest Jones, *The Life and Work of Sigmund Freud* (edited and abridged by Lionel Trilling and Steven Marcus) (Basic Books, New York, 1961), p. 527.

Page 141: "*I am only waiting for Moses which is due to appear in March, and then I need not be interested in any book of mine again until my next reincarnation.*"
Letter from Freud to Arnold Zweig, 5 March 1939, The International Psycho-Analytical Library, 84:1.

Page 142: "*Nearly all famous men are disappointing or bores, or both. Freud was neither; he had an aura, not of fame, but of greatness.*"
Leonard Woolf, *Downhill all the Way: an autobiography of the years 1919-1939* (Hogarth Press, London, 1967), p. 168.

Page 144: "*You promised me then you would help me when I could no longer carry on. It is only torture now and it has no longer any sense.*"
Ernest Jones, *The Life and Work of Sigmund Freud* (edited and abridged by Lionel Trilling and Steven Marcus) (Basic Books, New York, 1961), p.530.

Page 150: "*I'm pretty useless at psychology ... I feel a bit guilty at letting the family name down, but I'm sure that there are quite enough Freudian psychologists to go round.*"
Jack Freud, quoted in Sebastian Shakespeare and Olivia Cole, "Meet the Freuds," *Evening Standard*, April 17, 2009.

Sources for quotations

Page 9: Letter from Freud to the Mayor of Příbor-Freiberg, October 25, 1931, as appears in *Letters of Sigmund Freud 1873-1939*, edited by Ernst Freud, The Hogarth Press, London, 1960.

Page 14: Freud, Sigmund, *The Interpretation of Dreams*, Franz Deuticke, Vienna, 1909 second edition.

Page 29: Letter from Freud to Carl Koller, October 13, 1886, as appears in *Letters of Sigmund Freud 1873-1939*, edited by Ernst Freud, The Hogarth Press, London, 1960.

Page 43: Freud, Sigmund, *Civilization and Its Discontents*, Verlag, Austria, 1930.

Page 56: Freud, Sigmund, *The Interpretation of Dreams*, Franz Deuticke, Vienna, 1900 first editon.

Page 85: Freud, Sigmund, *Civilization and Its Discontents*, Verlag, Austria, 1930.

Page 107: Freud, Sigmund, paper entitled "A Difficulty in the Path of Psycho-Analysis," 1917, as appears in The Standard Edition of the *Complete Psychological Works of Sigmund Freud*, Volume XVII, General Editor James Strachey in collaboration with Anna Freud, assisted by Alix Strachey and Alan Tyson, 1999, Vintage, London.

Page 113: Postcard from Sigmund Freud to his wife Martha on July 12, 1912 during his stay at the sanatorium in Karlsbad, as appears in *Letters of Sigmund Freud 1873-1939* edited by Ernst Freud, The Hogarth Press, London, 1960.

Page 127: Letter from Sigmund Freud to Arnold Zweig, June 22, 1936, as appears in *Letters of Sigmund Freud 1873-1939*, edited by Ernst Freud, The Hogarth Press, London, 1960.

Page 134: Freud, Sigmund, paper entitled "A Complete Biographical Study," 1925, appears in The Standard Edition of the *Complete Psychological Works of Sigmund Freud*, Volume XX, General Editor James Strachey in collaboration with Anna Freud, assisted by Aliz Strachey and Alan Tyson, 1999, Vintage, London.

Page 141: Freud, Sigmund, "Beyond the Pleasure Principle," 1920, as appears in The Standard Edition of the *Complete Psychological Works of Sigmund Freud*, Volume XVIII, General Editor James Strachey in collaboration with Anna Freud, assisted by Alix Strachey and Alan Tyson, 1999, Vintage, London.

Page 149: Letter from Freud to Martha Bernays, August 18, 1883, as appears in *Letters of Sigmund Freud 1873-1939*, edited by Ernst Freud, The Hogarth Press, London, 1960.

Index

Picture Credits

The publishers would like to thank the following sources for their kind
permission to reproduce the pictures in this book.

AKG-Images: 7 (t), 8, 9, 10, 11 (t), 13 (b), 33, 35, 47, 48-49, 51, 55, 57,
58, 59, 66, 70, 71, 72, 73, 116, 133

Alamy: Chronicle: 55

Bridgeman Images: 30, 31, 44, 136-137, 143 (b), 144

Freud Museum: 6, 14, 16, 17, 18, 19, 20, 21, 22, 23, 24, 25, 26, 27, 36, 38
(left), 40, 41, 42, 43, 46, 47, 49, 50, 54, 56, 57, 58, 66, 73, 82-85, 87, 89-
91, 94, 98, 99, 104-109, 116-123, 127 (b), 134, 136-139, 142-143, 146-
147, 148, 154, 156 (r), 154, 166

Getty Images: 4, 28, 82, 127, 130, 134, 135, 151, 153; /114 Bettmann; /152

Dave M. Bennett; /65 Evening Standard; /56 Fine Art Images/Heritage
Images; /11 (b), 74 (b), 120, 122, 149 Hulton Archive; /3, 13 (t), 30, 40-
41, 54, 84, 87, 88-89, 100, 105, 115, 117 (t), 118 Imagno; /119 Keystone;
/126 Pictorial Parade; /139, 140 (l) Popperfoto; /104 Time Life Pictures/
Mansell/The LIFE Picture Collection

Library of Congress: 62-63, 68-69, 80,92-93

Mary Evans Picture Library: 27, 29 (left), 30, 101, 102

Private Collection: 110-111, 145-147

Topfoto: 34 (right), 141, 142, 143 The Granger Collection; /26, 29 (right)
Imagno; /6, 7 Ullstein Bild

Every effort has been made to acknowledge correctly and contact the
source and/or copyright holder of each picture and Carlton Books Limited
apologises for any unintentional errors or omissions, which will be
corrected in future editions of this book.